CA$H
CAB™

CA$H
CAB™

**A COLLECTION OF THE
BEST TRIVIA FROM THE HIT
DISCOVERY CHANNEL SERIES**

**FOREWORD BY
BEN BAILEY**

NAL NEW AMERICAN LIBRARY

NEW AMERICAN LIBRARY
Published by New American Library, a division of
Penguin Group (USA) Inc., 375 Hudson Street, New York, New York 10014, USA
Penguin Group (Canada), 90 Eglinton Avenue East, Suite 700, Toronto,
Ontario M4P 2Y3, Canada (a division of Pearson Penguin Canada Inc.)
Penguin Books Ltd., 80 Strand, London WC2R 0RL, England
Penguin Ireland, 25 St. Stephen's Green, Dublin 2,
Ireland (a division of Penguin Books Ltd.)
Penguin Group (Australia), 250 Camberwell Road, Camberwell, Victoria 3124,
Australia (a division of Pearson Australia Group Pty. Ltd.)
Penguin Books India Pvt. Ltd., 11 Community Centre, Panchsheel Park,
New Delhi - 110 017, India
Penguin Group (NZ), 67 Apollo Drive, Rosedale, Auckland 0632,
New Zealand (a division of Pearson New Zealand Ltd.)
Penguin Books (South Africa) (Pty.) Ltd., 24 Sturdee Avenue,
Rosebank, Johannesburg 2196, South Africa

Penguin Books Ltd., Registered Offices:
80 Strand, London WC2R 0RL, England

First published by New American Library,
a division of Penguin Group (USA) Inc.

First Printing, March 2012
10 9 8 7 6 5 4 3 2 1

 REGISTERED TRADEMARK—MARCA REGISTRADA

LIBRARY OF CONGRESS CATALOGING-IN-PUBLICATION DATA:

Cash Cab: a collection of the best trivia from the hit Discovery Channel series; foreword
by Ben Bailey.
p. cm.
ISBN 978-0-451-23590-9
1. Cash Cab (Television program)–Miscellanea.   2. Trivia.   3. Questions and Answers.
I. Discovery Communications, Inc.
PN1992.77.C36C37 2012
791.45'72–dc23   2011033390

Set in Century Schoolbook
Designed by Ginger Legato

Printed in the United States of America

Dedicated to the memory of

Tracy Cartwright.

E 33rd St
E 32nd St
E 31st St
E 30th St
W 29th St
W 28th St
E 29th St
E 28th St
W 27th St
Avenue Of The Americas
5th Ave
Madison Square Park
W 25th St
W 24th St
Chelsea Waterside Park
W 23rd St
W 22nd St
W 21st St
W 20th St
Park Ave S
Lexington Ave
E 26th St
E 25th St
E 24th St
E 23rd St
E 22nd St
E 21st St
E 23rd St
Gramercy Park
E 20th St
E 19th St
E 18th St
E 17th St
Avenue C
E River Dr
Marginal St
E River Piers
10th Ave
9th Ave
8th Ave
W 19th St
W 18th St
W 17th St
W 16th St
W 15th St
Broadway
5th Ave
Union Square
Irving Pl
Stuyvesant Square
E 15th St
E 14th St
W 14th St
7th Ave
1st Ave
E 14th St
E 15th St
10th Ave
Washington St
Hudson St
W 12th St
W 13th St
E 10th St
4th Ave
3rd Ave
University Pl
6th Ave
5th Ave
E 12th St
Avenue B
Avenue C
E 11th St
W 11th St
7th Ave S
E 10th St
E 9th St
E 8th St
Avenue A
Tompkins Square Park
E 8th St
12th Ave
Bank St
Perry St
W 10th St
Christopher St
MacDougal St
St Marks Pl
E 7th St
E 6th St
Loisaida Ave
W 3rd St
Mercer St
Lafayette St
E 5th St
Bowery
2nd Ave
E 4th St
E 3rd St
Morton St
7th Ave S
Bleecker St
E 2nd St
Clarkson St
Bleecker St
E Houston St
E 1st St
Varick St
6th Ave
W Broadway
Greene St
Broadway
Prince St
Elizabeth St
Chrystie St
Avenue Of The Immigrants
Stanton St
Rivington St
Ludlow St
Pitt St
Hudson St
Spring St
Allen St
Broome St
Broome St
Mott St
Mulberry St
Bowery
Essex St
Grand St
Grand St
Avenue Of The Americas
Lafayette St
Canal St
Eldridge St
E Broadway
Henry St
Laight St
Walker St
Baxter St
Hester St
Seward Park
Beach St
West St
N River Piers
Greenwich St
W Broadway
White St
Centre St
Madison St
Leonard St
Worth St
Thomas Paine Park
Catherine St
Cherry St
E River Piers
Duane St
Park Row
Chambers St
Governor Nelson A Rockefeller Park
N End Ave
Warren St
City Hall Park
Franklin D Roosevelt Dr
Manhattan Brg
Murray St
Church St
Frankfort St
Vesey St
Ann St
Pearl St
Brooklyn Brg
North Cove
Liberty St
Nassau St
William St
Pearl St
Front St
South St
Albany St
278

CONTENTS

E 32nd St
E 31st St
E 30th St
W 29th St
W 28th St
E 29th St
E 28th St
W 27th St
5th Ave
Avenue Of The Americas
Park Ave S
Lexington Ave
E River Dr
Marginal St
W 24th St
W 25th St
Madison Square Park
E 26th St
E 25th St
E 24th St
Chelsea Waterside Park
W 23rd St
W 22nd St
W 21st St
W 20th St
E 23rd St
E 22nd St
E 21st St
Gramercy Park
E 20th St
E 19th St
E 18th St
E 17th St
10th Ave
9th Ave
8th Ave
W 19th St
W 18th St
W 17th St
W 16th St
W 15th St
Broadway
Union Square
Irving Pl
Stuyvesant Square
E River Piers
Avenue C
W 14th St
E 15th St
E 14th St
1st Ave
Washington St
Hudson St
7th Ave
W 12th St
W 13th St
E 13th St
University Pl
4th Ave
3rd Ave
E 11th St
E 12th St
E 14th St
E 15th St
Avenue B
Avenue A
W 11th St
Bank St
Perry St
W 10th St
7th Ave S
6th Ave
5th Ave
E 10th St
E 9th St
E 8th St
St Marks Pl
E 7th St
Tompkins Square Park
E 8th St
Christopher St
MacDougal St
Mercer St
Lafayette St
W 3rd St
E 5th St
E 6th St
Loisaida Ave
Bowery
2nd Ave
E 4th St
E 3rd St
E 2nd St
Morton St
Bleecker St
Clarkson St
E Houston St
E 1st St
Varick St
Hudson St
W Broadway
Greene St
Prince St
Spring St
Elizabeth St
Chrystie St
Avenue Of The Immigrants
Stanton St
Rivington St
Ludlow St
Pitt St
Broome St
Grand St
Canal St
Mulberry St
Mott St
Allen St
Essex St
Laight St
Walker St
Baxter St
Hester St
Eldridge St
E Broadway
Henry St
Seward Park
Beach St
White St
Centre St
Madison St
West St
Greenwich St
Leonard St
Worth St
Thomas Paine Park
Catherine St
Cherry St
E River Piers
Duane St
Park Row
Chambers St
Warren St
City Hall Park
Franklin D Roosevelt Dr
Manhattan Brg
N End Ave
Murray St
Church St
Frankfort St
Vesey St
Ann St
Pearl St
Brooklyn Brg
North Cove
Liberty St
Nassau St
William St
Front St
South St
Albany St
278

FOREWORD BY BEN BAILEY

I went to college to be a stand-up comedian. That doesn't mean I went to Clown College. It just means that to do stand-up, you have to be a smart aleck—emphasis on "smart." You also have to be ready for whatever happens, because a lot of life is just chance.

For example, I got my start at The Comedy Store in Los Angeles, where I was hired to answer the phones. I was in the green room one night, making the other comedians in the room laugh so hard that the guy doing bookings got me a gig. Glad I went to college!

However, I did not go to college to drive a taxi. (Although I did drive a limo once, it was entirely without any formal training.) Still, being able to drive a cab was among the requirements for hosting *Cash Cab*. This was unexpected, considering that it was just a big open audition—kind of like open mic night at a comedy club.

So I had to go to Taxi School. Because the Cash Cab is a real New York City taxi and New York taxis are regulated by something called the Taxi and Limousine Commission, which is very, very particular about who gets to drive a cab in New York. Here's what you have to do to get a hack license in New York. (Hack is a very old word for taxicab; it comes from hackney, which is a horse-drawn vehicle kept for hire. But a hack is also someone who produces dull, unoriginal work, and as a comedian, well, that just hurts.)

- Be 19 years or older and a legal resident of the United States with a Social Security card and a driver's license.
- Take a six-hour defensive driving class.
- Get a signed medical history form and fill out a long application.
- Attend Taxi School—at your own expense— for either 24 hours or 80 hours, depending on how much you think you need to learn.
- Pass an English proficiency exam. (Because English is my first language, I was actually one of the few who didn't have to do that part.)
- Pass the Taxi and Limousine Commission exam, which includes questions about New York geography, map reading, and a very long list of rules and regulations.
- Pay $245 in various fees (plus the cost of Taxi School, which can range from $195 to $325).

I was the only white guy at Taxi School. Everyone else was either Middle Eastern or African. The first day, I came in at the front of the room and everyone sat up straight and opened their notebooks. They thought I was the teacher.

They were all astonished when I went to the back of the room and took my seat.

Because I passed my Taxi School final exam with flying colors, I know that cabdrivers really aren't supposed to talk to passengers, operate flashing lights and music inside their cab, ask hard quiz questions (and know all the answers), and keep track of everyone's score while also driving in New York City traffic. So I'll let you in on a secret: I don't.

I have assistants—the Vanna Whites of *Cash Cab*—who sit next to me in the front seat. After a group of contestants gets in the Cash Cab and I reveal my secret identity, I pull over and let one of the Vannas into my cab. She gets the contestants to sign a release form, and also operates the lights and music and keeps track of how much money they've won.

I do have to operate the meter, because the Taxi and Limousine Commission insists that there be a record of the trip. But *Cash Cab* contestants don't pay for their ride. In fact, the Staten Island Ferry and Cash Cab are the only two free rides in New York. Despite that, people have sometimes reacted a bit weird to the offer of a free cab ride and the chance to win some money.

Some people just ask me to turn the music down and pay no attention at all to what I'm saying. One woman kept reading her BlackBerry and got irritated that the ceiling was lighting up and music was playing, and made it clear she couldn't be bothered. A few people have actually started crying; generally, they're from out of town.

People also sometimes act weird when they get kicked out of the cab for getting too many questions wrong. I don't know why they're so upset, because *they just got a free cab ride.* But I've had plenty of people get a question wrong and get embarrassed, and then pissed off, and then start contesting the answer.

I picked up two guys in the East Village once and they went for the video bonus. It was a figure skating question— "Featuring a forward takeoff, this jump is named for the Norwegian ice skater who first performed it in 1882"— and the video showed someone doing the jump. One guy says to the other, "I think it's the axel," and other guy says, "Yeah, yeah, it's the axel," and they keep on like that until I say, "I'm going to need an answer." And the guy who was giving the answers says "salchow." I said, "No, it's the axel." (These are the moments I practice my deadpan for.) He got really pissed off, screamed the f-word, and punched the taxi partition with both fists. I said, "No punching the cab, buddy." And, just like a little kid, he said, "I didn't." (That game actually aired, but you didn't get to see that part on TV.)

Despite all that, I really love being the host of *Cash Cab*. I get a lot of positive feedback about the show from the fans everywhere I go. They're all so kind and supportive and have really nice things to say. In fact, it's hard to have a bad day anymore because there's always someone coming up to me telling me how much they love the show.

I also have a couple of Emmys, which are really just cool statues of an angel shooting a free throw. I keep them on my piano, which I am learning how to play.

Reading this book is just like being on *Cash Cab*, so I hope you are having an Emmy-worthy experience right now. Inside, you'll find thirty quizzes of various lengths and forty-four boxes with information about New York, taxis, and taxis in New York. You can play the game at home by yourself or with friends. Or take it to a bar and try to hear each other over the noise. Or, for a truly authentic experience, take it along on your next taxi ride. And please be nice to your cabdriver—he is, after all, a graduate of Taxi School.

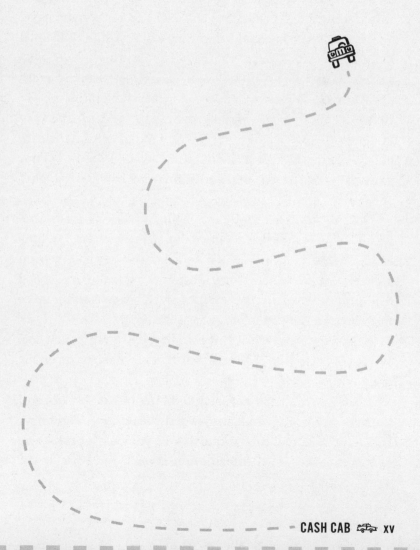

W 31st St
E 33rd St
E 32nd St
E 31st St
E 30th St
W 29th St
W 28th St
E 29th St
E 28th St
W 27th St
5th Ave
Avenue Of The Americas
Madison Square Park
W 25th St
W 24th St
Chelsea Waterside
Park Ave S
Lexington Ave
E 26th St
E 25th St
E 24th St
W 23rd St
W 22nd St
W 21st St
W 20th St
E 23rd St
E 22nd St
E 21st St
Gramercy Park
E 20th St
10th Ave
9th Ave
8th Ave
W 19th St
W 18th St
W 17th St
W 16th St
W 15th St
Broadway
E 19th St
E 18th St
E 17th St
Avenue C
E River Dr
Marginal St
E River Piers
Union Square
Irving Pl
E 15th St
E 14th St
Stuyvesant Square
7th Ave
W 14th St
W 13th St
W 12th St
E 13th St
1st Ave
E 14th St
E 15th St
Washington St
Hudson St
W 11th St
6th Ave
5th Ave
University Pl
4th Ave
3rd Ave
E 11th St
E 12th St
Avenue B
Avenue C
Bank St
Perry St
W 10th St
7th Ave S
E 10th St
E 9th St
E 8th St
Avenue A
Tompkins Square Park
E 8th St
Christopher
MacDougal St
St Marks Pl
E 7th St
E 6th St
W 3rd St
Mercer St
Lafayette St
E 5th St
Loisaida Ave
Bowery
2nd Ave
E 4th St
E 3rd St
Morton St
Bleecker St
E 2nd St
Clarkson St
E Houston St
E 1st St
Varick St
W Broadway
Greene St
Stanton St
Prince St
Rivington St
Elizabeth St
Chrystie St
Pitt St
Spring St
Avenue Of The Immigrants
Ludlow St
Allen St
9
Broome St
Mott St
Broome St
Grand St
Grand St
Essex St
Canal St
Mulberry St
Eldridge St
E Broadway
Henry St
Laight St
Walker St
Baxter St
Hester St
Seward Park
Beach St
White St
Madison St
N River Piers
West St
Greenwich St
Centre St
Leonard St
Market St
Cherry St
Worth St
E River Piers
Duane St
Thomas Paine Park
Catherine St
Chambers St
Park Row
Governor Nelson A Rockefeller Park
Warren St
N End Ave
City Hall Park
Franklin D Roosevelt Dr
Murray St
Frankfort St
Manhattan Brg
Vesey St
Church St
Ann St
Brooklyn Brg
North Cove
Pearl St
Liberty St
Nassau St
William St
Front St
South St
Albany St
278

ACKNOWLEDGMENTS

A big thanks to the following people: Beth Adelman, who pulled this whole book together and found out everything there is to know about taxis and New York; our agent, Erin Niumata, at Folio Literary Management and our editor, Mark Chait, at New American Library; and the folks at Lion TV for all their work writing and producing the show.

E 33rd St
E 32nd St
E 31st St
E 30th St
W 29th St
W 28th St
E 29th St
E 28th St
W 27th St
5th Ave
E River Dr
W 24th St
W 25th St
Madison Square Park
Park Ave S
Lexington Ave
E 26th St
E 25th St
W 23rd St
W 22nd St
E 24th St
Avenue Of The Americas
Broadway
E 23rd St
W 21st St
W 20th St
E 22nd St
E 21st St
10th Ave
9th Ave
8th Ave
W 19th St
Gramercy Park
E 20th St
Avenue C
W 18th St
W 17th St
E 19th St
E 18th St
W 16th St
E 17th St
W 15th St
7th Ave
Union Square
Stuyvesant Square
Irving Pl
W 14th St
E 15th St
E 14th St
Washington St
Hudson St
W 12th St
W 13th St
E 13th St
University Pl
4th Ave
3rd Ave
1st Ave
E 14th St
E 15th St
E 12th St
Avenue B
Avenue C
W 11th St
E 11th St
7th Ave S
E 10th St
E 9th St
E 8th St
Avenue A
Bank St
Perry St
W 10th St
MacDougal St
5th Ave
Tompkins Square Park
E 8th St
St Marks Pl
E 7th St
E 6th St
Christopher St
Mercer St
Lafayette St
Bowery
2nd Ave
E 5th St
Loisaida Ave
Avenue D
W 3rd St
E 4th St
Morton St
Bleecker St
E 3rd St
E 2nd St
Clarkson St
Varick St
E Houston St
E 1st St
Stanton St
W Broadway
Greene St
Prince St
Elizabeth St
Chrystie St
Avenue Of The Immigrants
Rivington St
Pitt St
Hudson St
Spring St
Mulberry St
Allen St
Ludlow St
Essex St
Broome St
Grand St
Mott St
Eldridge St
E Broadway
Henry St
Canal St
Laight St
Hester St
Seward Park
Beach St
Walker St
Baxter St
West St
White St
Centre St
Madison St
N River Piers
Greenwich St
Leonard St
Worth St
Cherry St
E River Piers
Duane St
Thomas Paine Park
Park Row
Catherine St
Chambers St
Governor Nelson A Rockefeller Park
Warren St
City Hall Park
N End Ave
Murray St
Church St
Frankfort St
Franklin D Roosevelt Dr
Manhattan Brg
Vesey St
Ann St
Brooklyn Brg
North Cove
Pearl St
Liberty St
Nassau St
William St
Albany St
Front St
South St
278
9

HOW TO PLAY *CASH CAB*

H ere are the *Cash Cab* rules of the road.

The game lasts as long as your cab ride—which in this case is based on a formula that's so complicated we can't explain it. The first batch of questions will be worth $50 each, the next batch $100 each, and the remaining questions $200 each.

The questions are going to get harder as the dollar values go up. This is how life works. Did you expect it to be any different?

What happens if you get one wrong? That's one strike. And it doesn't take a genius to know that three strikes means you're out. Get out of the cab; your ride is done and you leave with no money. And no pride.

What if you're playing alone? You'd have to look at the answers as you go along to know when you've got three strikes. And no matter how honest and upstanding you are, if you look at the answer to one question, you're going to see the answer to the next question—the question that hasn't been asked yet, the question you shouldn't be seeing the answer to. So now what?

You can play this any way you like, but here are a couple of suggestions.

1. Find a friend to play with.
2. Play the game through, then look at the answers. When you get to three strikes, stop adding up your money.
3. Just add up your money and don't worry about the strikes.

Or do whatever you want. Because if you're playing alone, no one will know.

You are allowed to ask for help—just not too much of it. You win big in *Cash Cab* by knowing a lot of stuff. But if you're really stumped, you get one Mobile Shout-Out and one Street Shout-Out. That's one phone call to ask your smart-aleck friend the answer. And one live human being you can consult with—maybe someone else in the room, or for a real Street Shout-Out, open the window and ask someone you see walking by who appears to be sober. (The Web does not count as a live person, so no fair looking something up. Checking the answer page also doesn't count as a Shout-Out. That's just peeking at the answers.)

We're bound to hit a few red lights along the way (Ben will tell you when you do), and that's when you'll face the Red Light Challenge. It's a single question with multiple answers. Sometimes you have to get them all right (like name all seven of Snow White's dwarfs), sometimes just some of them. A Red Light Challenge is worth $250, but to earn that you have to get all the answers right. So if the

question asks for, say, five of the seven dwarfs, you need five—four gets you nothing. The good part is that any answer you get wrong won't count as a strike, so you can just shout out answers as they pop into your head. You've got 30 seconds to get them all. (If you're playing by yourself, don't cheat.)

When you get to your destination, you can keep the cash you've earned so far and use it to buy yourself another cab ride. Or you can bet it all on one Double or Nothing Bonus Question. You know that on the television version of *Cash Cab* this is always a Video Bonus. But some of you are reading this on a content delivery device that doesn't have video (yes, a printed book is a content delivery device). So we'll skip the video and just stick with questions you can picture in your head. This part is called Ben's Double or Nothing Bonus. We double dare you.

Are you ready? Time to play *Cash Cab*.

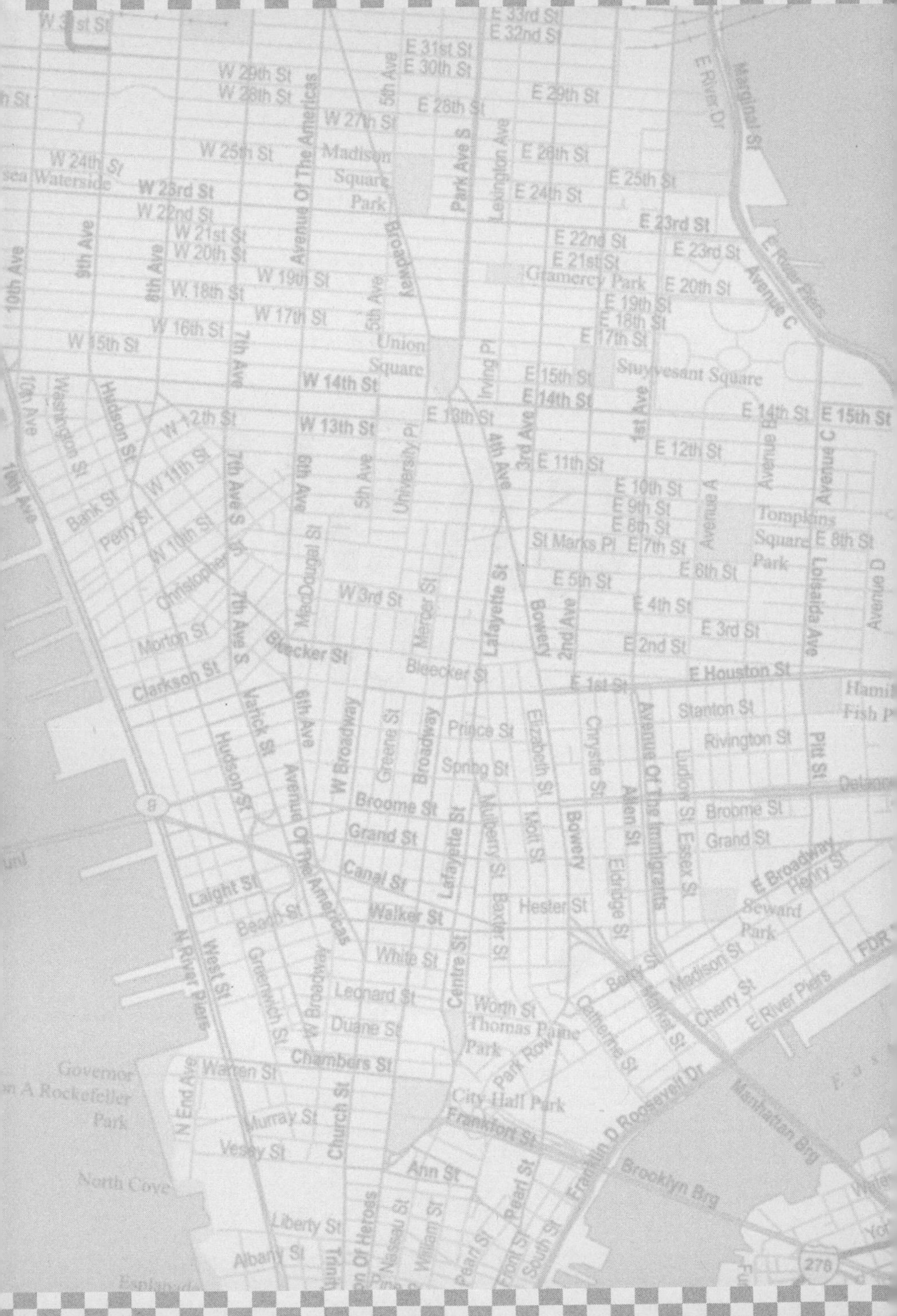

E 33rd St
E 32nd St
E 31st St
E 30th St
W 29th St
W 28th St
E 29th St
E 28th St
W 27th St
5th Ave
Avenue Of The Americas
Park Ave S
Lexington Ave
E River Dr
Marginal St
W 25th St
Madison
Square
Park
E 26th St
W 24th St
Waterside
E 25th St
W 23rd St
E 24th St
W 22nd St
E 23rd St
W 21st St
W 20th St
E 22nd St
E 21st St
E 23rd St
10th Ave
9th Ave
8th Ave
W 19th St
Broadway
Gramercy Park
E 20th St
Avenue C
E River Piers
W 18th St
5th Ave
E 19th St
W 17th St
E 18th St
W 16th St
E 17th St
W 15th St
Union
Square
Irving Pl
7th Ave
E 15th St
Stuyvesant Square
W 14th St
E 14th St
10th Ave
Washington St
Hudson St
W 12th St
E 13th St
1st Ave
E 14th St
E 15th St
W 13th St
4th Ave
Avenue B
Avenue C
University Pl
3rd Ave
E 12th St
W 11th St
E 11th St
7th Ave S
6th Ave
5th Ave
E 10th St
E 9th St
Bank St
Avenue A
Tompkins
Square
Park
E 8th St
Perry St
W 10th St
E 8th St
St Marks Pl
E 7th St
Christopher
MacDougal St
Mercer St
E 6th St
Loisaida Ave
Avenue D
Lafayette St
E 5th St
W 3rd St
Bowery
E 4th St
2nd Ave
7th Ave S
E 3rd St
Morton St
Bleecker St
E 2nd St
Bleecker St
Clarkson St
E Houston St
E 1st St
Varick St
6th Ave
Stanton St
Hudson St
W Broadway
Greene St
Broadway
Prince St
Elizabeth St
Chrystie St
Avenue Of The Immigrants
Rivington St
Pitt St
Ludlow St
Spring St
Allen St
Avenue Of The Americas
Broome St
Mulberry St
Mott St
Essex St
Broome St
9
Grand St
Bowery
Grand St
Lafayette St
Canal St
Baxter St
Eldridge St
E Broadway
Perry St
Laight St
Hester St
Walker St
Seward
Park
Beach St
FDR
N River Piers
West St
Greenwich St
White St
Centre St
Madison St
Market St
Cherry St
E River Piers
Leonard St
Worth St
Thomas Paine
Park
Duane St
Catherine St
Chambers St
Park Row
Governor
Park
Warren St
N End Ave
Church St
City Hall Park
Franklin D Roosevelt Dr
Manhattan Brg
Murray St
Frankfort St
Vesey St
Ann St
Pearl St
Brooklyn Brg
North Cove
Liberty St
Nassau St
William St
Pearl St
Front St
South St
Albany St
278

SECOND AVENUE AND ST. MARKS PLACE TO NINTH AVENUE AND 22ND STREET (22 BLOCKS)

These questions are worth $50 each.

1. In the novel *Don Quixote,* what swiveling structures are mistaken for giants with arms "nearly two leagues long"?
2. Though it may be highly illogical, what actor titled his two autobiographies *I Am Spock* and *I Am Not Spock*?
3. Meaning "liver inflammation" in Greek, what disease can be caused by uncooked oysters and unsanitary tattoo artists?
4. Boasting a ham of a mascot, what rhyming supermarket chain first introduced Americans to self-service groceries?

THE FIRST TAXIS

The first gasoline-powered taxis hit the streets of New York in 1907, when Harry N. Allen imported sixty-five automobiles from France and started the New York Taxicab Company. Before that, the horsepower in taxicabs was the literal kind—horse-drawn buggies known as hansom cabs. Allen, a thirty-year-old New York businessman and typical yuppie, decided to start his own business after a hansom cabdriver charged him and his lady friend $5 for a three-quarter-mile trip home from a restaurant. That's about $110 in today's money, so it was a lot.

Allen sent his taxis to the cab stands at major hotels and instructed his drivers to be polite and honest—apparently a new idea at the time. Within a year he had seven hundred red-and-green-paneled cabs on the streets of New York.

But just as Allen was getting started, he was hit with a labor strike. The cabbies didn't like the fees he was charging for the use of the cars and their uniforms, and they wanted free gasoline because the price of gas was too high. (Nothing changes, does it?) Allen hired strikebreakers, the strike became violent, and Allen was forced out of the business by the mounting legal costs.

These questions are worth $100 each.

1. Similar to its linguistic spouse POTUS, the acronym FLOTUS refers to what important figure on the Washington, D.C., scene?
2. What pale yellow liquid component of blood is often collected from college students in need of quick cash?

3. What mythological creature, finally slayed by Hercules, grew two new heads for every one that was cut off?
4. Familiar to night owls, what infomercial guru do we have to thank for the Veg-O-Matic and the Pocket Fisherman?

These questions are worth $200 each.

1. A childhood rite of passage, the MMR vaccine protects against measles, mumps, and what?
2. What is the avian-inspired slang word Canadians use to refer to their one-dollar coin?

RED LIGHT CHALLENGE

We're stopped at a red light, so it's time for a Red Light Challenge. Remember, this is worth $250.
According to the Encarta Encyclopedia, *what are the five most popular types of red wine grapes in the United States? You have 30 seconds to name all five.*

3. Once the center of the Khmer Empire, the Angkor Wat temple is featured on what Asian country's flag?

4. Name the famed ship that's been escorting tourists to within spitting distance of Niagara Falls for more than one hundred years.

Ben's Double or Nothing Bonus

As suggested by a children's song, this bird roosts in the old gum trees of its native Australia. With a call that echoes human laughter, what is the name of this noisy bird from Down Under?

$50 questions

1. Windmills
2. Leonard Nimoy
3. Hepatitis
4. Piggly Wiggly

$100 questions

1. First Lady of the United States
   (POTUS is President of the United States)
2. Plasma
3. Hydra
4. Ron Popeil

$200 questions

1. Rubella
2. Loonie

Red Light Challenge

Zinfandel
Cabernet Sauvignon
Grenache
Merlot
Pinot Noir

3. Cambodia
4. Maid of the Mist

Ben's Double or Nothing Bonus

Kookaburra

AND THE ANSWERS ARE . . .

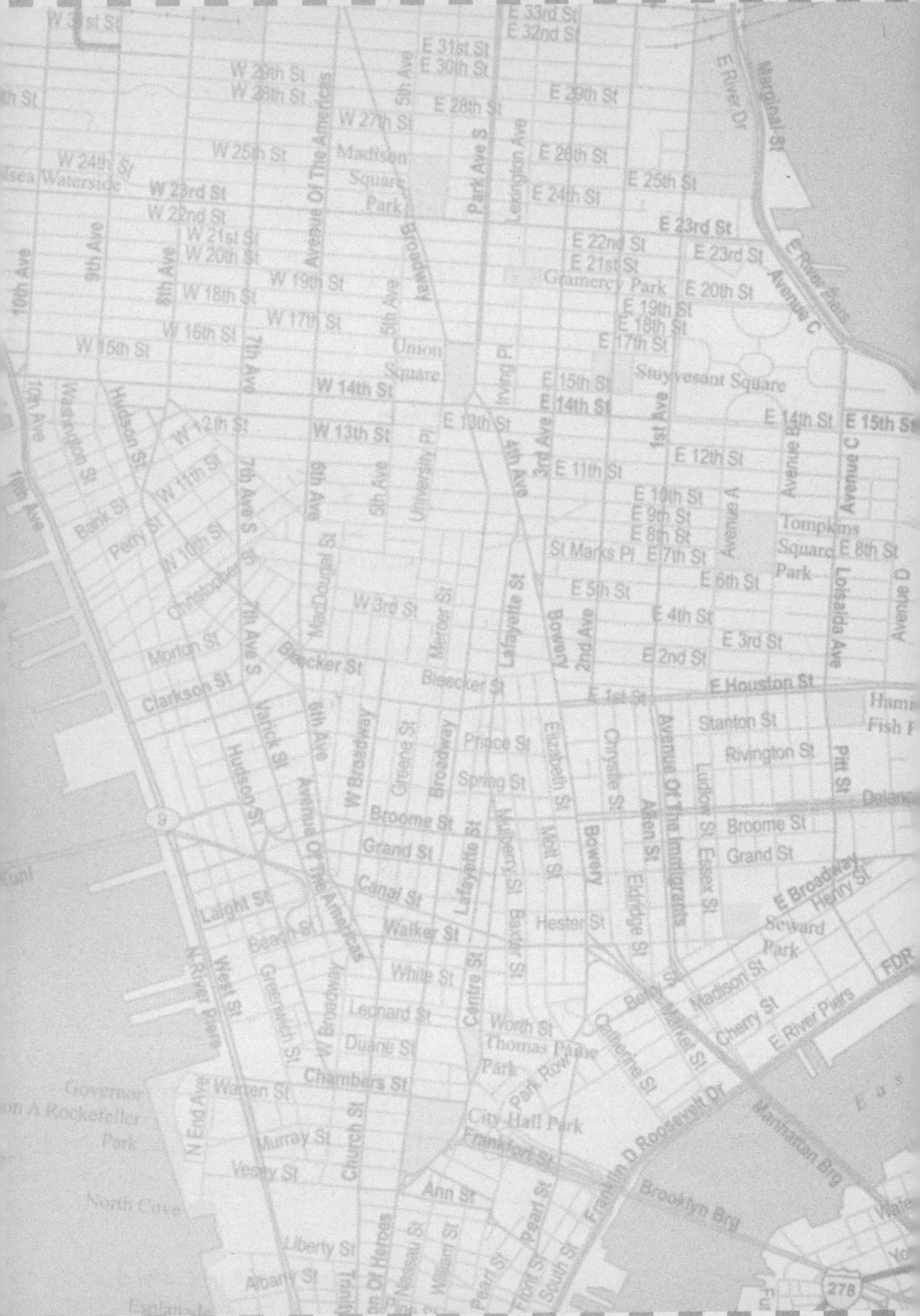

E 33rd St
E 32nd St
E 31st St
E 30th St
W 29th St
W 28th St
E 29th St
E 28th St
W 27th St
5th Ave
Avenue Of The Americas
E River Dr
Marginal St
W 25th St
Madison Square Park
Park Ave S
Lexington Ave
E 26th St
W 24th St
Waterside
E 25th St
W 23rd St
E 24th St
W 22nd St
E 23rd St
W 21st St
W 20th St
E 22nd St
E 21st St
E 23rd St
10th Ave
9th Ave
8th Ave
Broadway
W 19th St
Gramercy Park
E 20th St
W 18th St
E River Piers
Avenue C
W 17th St
5th Ave
E 19th St
E 18th St
W 16th St
E 17th St
W 15th St
Union Square
Irving Pl
Stuyvesant Square
7th Ave
W 14th St
E 15th St
E 14th St
E 14th St
E 15th St
10th Ave
Washington St
Hudson St
W 12th St
E 10th St
W 13th St
University Pl
4th Ave
3rd Ave
1st Ave
Avenue B
Avenue C
E 12th St
E 11th St
W 11th St
7th Ave S
6th Ave
5th Ave
E 10th St
E 9th St
E 8th St
Avenue A
Tompkins Square Park
Bank St
Perry St
W 10th St
St Marks Pl
E 7th St
E 8th St
MacDougal St
Christopher
E 6th St
Loisaida Ave
Avenue D
W 3rd St
Mercer St
Lafayette St
E 5th St
Bowery
2nd Ave
E 4th St
Morton St
7th Ave S
E 3rd St
Bleecker St
E 2nd St
Bleecker St
Clarkson St
E Houston St
E 1st St
Varick St
6th Ave
W Broadway
Greene St
Broadway
Prince St
Elizabeth St
Chrystie St
Avenue Of The Immigrants
Stanton St
Rivington St
Pitt St
Hudson St
Spring St
Ludlow St
Delancey
Avenue Of The Americas
Broome St
Mulberry St
Mott St
Bowery
Allen St
Broome St
Grand St
Lafayette St
Essex St
Grand St
Canal St
Baxter St
Eldridge St
E Broadway
Henry St
Laight St
Walker St
Hester St
Seward Park
Beach St
Centre St
FDR
N River Piers
West St
Greenwich St
W Broadway
White St
Madison St
Leonard St
Worth St
Market St
Cherry St
E River Piers
Duane St
Thomas Paine Park
Catherine St
Chambers St
Park Row
Governor
Rockefeller Park
N End Ave
Warren St
City Hall Park
Franklin D Roosevelt Dr
Manhattan Brg
Murray St
Frankfort St
Church St
Vesey St
Ann St
Pearl St
Brooklyn Brg
North Cove
Nassau St
William St
Pearl St
Front St
South St
Liberty St
Albany St
278

33RD STREET AND NINTH
TO 75TH STREET AND WEST END AVENUE
(40 BLOCKS)

These questions are worth $50 each.

1. Also known as a "dolphin fish" although it has no relation to Flipper, what tasty ocean dweller has a name that means "strong-strong" in Hawaiian?
2. Name the sound-sensitive on-off device invented by the same company that brought us the Chia Pet?
3. Either metal or rubber, what are the studs on the bottom of soccer shoes known as?
4. A 1958 experiment with a tape recorder gave birth to a trio of cartoon chipmunks named Alvin, Simon, and what?
5. A staple of British pub grub, "bangers and mash" refers to mashed potatoes and what?
6. What famous waterway connecting the Atlantic and Pacific Oceans opened in 1914?

RED LIGHT CHALLENGE 1

Saudi Arabia shares its land borders with seven Middle Eastern nations. Name five of these Saudi neighbors. You have 30 seconds.

These questions are worth $100 each.

1. The Marquess of Queensberry Rules frown upon wrestling and hugging; they regulate what sport?
2. Known formally as "cerumen," what substance in your head is either flaky or gooey, depending on your genes?
3. On TV's *Star Trek: The Next Generation,* what ominous catchphrase is uttered by the resource-hungry Borg?
4. In politics, what term for a pet project alludes to a system once used to put ID on pigs and cattle?
5. Popular with white-haired ladies, in what Chinese game do players build suits from thirteen or sixteen tiles?
6. What strong synthetic fiber invented in the 1960s is associated with bulletproof vests?

THE ANSONIA

This trip takes us right past the Ansonia, a gorgeous turn-of-the-century (the previous one) apartment building on Broadway and 73rd Street. It's always been a favorite of opera singers and orchestra conductors, because it's a short walk to Lincoln Center. Enrico Caruso, Sergei Rachmaninoff, Igor Stravinsky, Arturo Toscanini, Gustav Mahler, Lily Pons, and Ezio Pinza all lived there. So did Babe Ruth—who was an opera fan.

The Ansonia started out as a luxury residential hotel, built by William Earle Dodge Stokes, who was the heir to a copper fortune. The residents lived in huge apartments with sweeping views along Broadway. There was a central kitchen where professional chefs cooked for everyone, and serving kitchens on every floor, so the residents could dine in their own apartments.

Dodge had the idea to build a kind of self-sufficient luxury commune. To that end, he established a small farm on the roof of the hotel. The building had a spacious cattle elevator, so dairy cows could be taken up there. The roof farm also included ducks, goats, and chickens. Every day, a bellhop delivered free fresh eggs to all the tenants.

But despite the barnyard in the sky, the Ansonia was all class. It had the usual array of tearooms, restaurants, and a grand ballroom, plus Turkish baths in the basement and a fountain in the lobby with live seals.

In the 1960s and '70s, the Turkish baths became the Continental Baths, a gay bathhouse that offered superb entertainment (Sarah Vaughan sang there, as did many opera stars) and hot steam. Bette Midler started her career at the Continental Baths, with Barry Manilow as her accompanist.

In 1977, the baths became Plato's Retreat, a famous (or infamous, depending on your point of view) heterosexual swing club. Today, it's just an underground parking lot.

These questions are worth $200 each.

1. First distilled by the Spanish in the 1500s, what liquor is made from the succulent agave plant?
2. In 1928, Alexander Fleming discovered what medicine used to fight bacterial infections?

RED LIGHT CHALLENGE 2

This Red Light Challenge takes us back to the days of high school chemistry. Name six of the nine elements on the Periodic Table that end with the letters O-N.
This is worth $250.

3. Name the controversial former owner of baseball's Cincinnati Reds who was often suspended for her racial slurs.
4. In 1996, what rap artist released a posthumous album under the alias Makaveli?
5. Also the name of Steve Jobs' daughter, what Apple computer flop was introduced in 1983 for the whopping price of ten thousand bucks?
6. What denomination of Protestantism was founded in the sixteenth century by a Frenchman whose tombstone reads only "J.C."?

Ben's Double or Nothing Bonus

Due to its venomous, lethal bite, this African reptile is widely considered to be the world's deadliest snake. Not to be confused with a type of Cuban dance, what is the name of this carnivorous cousin of the cobra?

AND THE ANSWERS ARE . . .

$50 questions

1. Mahi-mahi
2. The Clapper
3. Cleats
4. Theodore
5. Sausages
6. Panama Canal

Red Light Challenge 1

Iraq
Jordan
Kuwait
Oman
Qatar
United Arab Emirates
Yemen

$100 questions

1. Boxing
2. Ear wax
3. "Resistance is futile."
4. Earmark
5. Mahjong
6. Kevlar

$200 questions

1. Tequila
2. Penicillin

Red Light Challenge 2

Argon
Boron
Carbon
Iron
Krypton
Neon
Radon
Silicon
Xenon

3. Marge Schott
4. Tupac Shakur
5. Lisa
6. Calvinism (named for John Calvin)

Ben's Double or Nothing Bonus

Mamba

W 31st St
E 33rd St
E 32nd St
E 31st St
E 30th St
W 29th St
W 28th St
E 29th St
E 28th St
W 27th St
Avenue Of The Americas
5th Ave
E River Dr
Marginal St
W 26th St
Madison Square Park
Park Ave S
Lexington Ave
E 26th St
W 24th St
E 25th St
W 23rd St
E 24th St
W 22nd St
E 23rd St
W 21st St
W 20th St
E 22nd St
E 21st St
10th Ave
9th Ave
8th Ave
Broadway
Gramercy Park
E 20th St
W 19th St
E River Piers
Avenue C
W 18th St
E 19th St
E 18th St
W 17th St
W 16th St
E 17th St
W 15th St
Union Square
Irving Pl
Stuyvesant Square
E 15th St
W 14th St
E 14th St
7th Ave
Washington St
Hudson St
W 12th St
W 13th St
University Pl
E 13th St
4th Ave
3rd Ave
E 14th St
E 15th St
1st Ave
E 12th St
Avenue B
W 11th St
6th Ave
E 11th St
E 10th St
E 9th St
E 8th St
Avenue A
Tompkins Square Park
E 8th St
Bank St
Perry St
7th Ave S
W 10th St
St Marks Pl
E 7th St
Christopher St
MacDougal St
E 6th St
W 3rd St
Mercer St
Lafayette St
E 5th St
E 4th St
Loisaida Ave
Bowery
2nd Ave
E 3rd St
Morton St
Bleecker St
E 2nd St
Clarkson St
Bleecker St
E Houston St
E 1st St
Varick St
Stanton St
Hudson St
W Broadway
Greene St
Prince St
Elizabeth St
Chrystie St
Avenue Of The Immigrants
Rivington St
Pitt St
Spring St
Ludlow St
Broome St
Allen St
Broome St
Mott St
Grand St
Grand St
Mulberry St
Essex St
E Broadway
Henry St
Canal St
Eldridge St
Laight St
Hester St
Seward Park
Beach St
Walker St
Baxter St
Centre St
White St
Madison St
West St
Greenwich St
Leonard St
Cherry St
E River Piers
N River Piers
Worth St
Catherine St
Duane St
Thomas Paine Park
Chambers St
Park Row
Governor Nelson A Rockefeller Park
N End Ave
Warren St
City Hall Park
Franklin D Roosevelt Dr
Manhattan Brg
Murray St
Frankfort St
Church St
Vesey St
Ann St
Brooklyn Brg
North Cove
Pearl St
Liberty St
Nassau St
William St
South St
Front St
Albany St
278

BATTERY PARK TO
ROCKEFELLER CENTER
(78 BLOCKS)

These questions are worth $50 each.

1. What is the official name for a group of lions?
2. A staple of sitcoms, what artificial TV sound effect made its debut in 1950 on *The Hank McCune Show*?
3. Cohiba, Dutch Master, and Padron are all brands of what?
4. Introduced in 1975, what sizzling candy ran a full-page ad assuring parents it didn't make your stomach explode?
5. Fond of long legs and luscious eyelashes, the Qahtani tribe of Saudi Arabia holds an annual pageant for what four-legged desert dwellers?
6. With a smell like rotten eggs, what chemical element puts the "stink" in stink bombs?

7. From a Latin word meaning "caught in the act," what type of public declaration is associated with both Karl Marx and the Unabomber?

RED LIGHT CHALLENGE 1

Time for a Red Light Challenge. Remember, this is worth $250.

From 1994 to 2010, six Disney movies have migrated to the Great White Way to become Broadway musicals. You have 30 seconds to name at least four of these Disneyfied shows. Go!

8. As of 2007, Starbucks cafés are now "verboten" from what ancient palace complex in Beijing?

9. If you want to "beat the rap," you should probably know that RAP stands for "Record of Arrests and" what?

10. Missing her shot at preventing World War I, what gunslinger safely blasted a cigarette from the hand of Kaiser Wilhelm the Second?

SIX FAMOUS EX-CABBIES

Being a cabbie can be a great career—you can sit down all day and still get out and see the sights—but a lot of people have used it as a way to make money while they work on something else. Here are six famous people who used to drive a cab.

Larry David

After watching a zillion episodes of *Seinfeld* and *Curb Your Enthusiasm,* one can imagine Larry David as the rudest, most opinionated New York cabbie ever. But in a good way.

David Mamet

The Pulitzer Prize–winning playwright says his stint as a Chicago cabdriver was on-the-job training for his career as a writer.

Jimmy Smits

In the early 1980s, Jimmy Smits acted in off-Broadway plays and drove a cab on the overnight shift. That lasted until he received the pilot script for a new show producer Steven Bochco was developing called *L.A. Law.*

Danny Glover

In 1999, the actor used his leverage as a former San Francisco cabdriver to raise awareness about cabbies sometimes not picking up African-American passengers.

Philip Glass

Philip Glass was just another Juilliard-trained composer struggling to make a living in New York City when he drove a taxi. He said he loved the job because he was free to let his mind wander. It was behind the wheel of a cab that Glass worked on *Einstein on the Beach*, his most famous opera.

These questions are worth $100 each.

1. The world's best-selling domestic robot, Roomba, is a product designed specifically to do what task?

2. What modern-day Turkish city was originally named for Roman emperor Constantine?

3. Containing the hormone estrogen, what trendy vegetable protein has been linked to lower fertility rates in males?

4. To the chagrin of detectives Down Under, what marsupial's fingerprints are almost identical to humans?

5. The enemy of Snidely Whiplash, what cartoon character was accused of mocking Canadian Mounties?

6. In 1997, the USS *Yorktown* was paralyzed when its computer tried to divide a number by what digit?

7. In the logical lingo of the logging industry, what do you call a female lumberjack?

8. A staple of brunch, what cocktail consists of four parts orange juice and six parts champagne?

9. Who made the fifty jewel-encrusted eggs presented to Russian Tsars between 1885 and 1917?

10. What table game features twenty-eight rectangular pieces called "bones" marked with dots called "pips"?

RED LIGHT CHALLENGE 2

This Red Light Challenge is brought to you by the great nation of CashCabistan. Name four of the seven nations in the world that end with the suffix "stan." This is worth $250.

These questions are worth $200 each.

1. Due to his fondness for them, what author's name is commonly used to identify cats with extra toes?
2. Once used to pave airport runways, what road surface was invented by E. Purnell Hooley in 1901?
3. From the French word for "untie," what literary term refers to the final part of a story where everything is resolved?
4. A Shoshone Indian from Idaho served as the model for what famous woman on the U.S. Golden Dollar coin?
5. According to comedian Chris Rock, what intoxicating section of a "gentleman's club" offers plenty of liquor but absolutely no sex?
6. One row in front of Sigmund Freud, what Swiss psychiatrist is depicted on the iconic album cover of the Beatles' *Sgt. Pepper's Lonely Hearts Club Band*?

RED LIGHT CHALLENGE 3

Another red light, another Red Light Challenge. Yum! Brands is a Fortune 500 company that operates six fast-food franchises in the United States. Name four of these Yum-owned (Yummy?) franchises.

7. What city was nearly destroyed by the massive 1666 fire that started in a bakery on Pudding Lane?

8. In Greek mythology, what unfortunate nymph is able only to repeat words spoken by others?

9. What environmentally conscious Dr. Seuss character claims to "speak for the trees"?

10. Hung to dry for two months, hákarl (you pronounce that *HAW-karl*) is a fermented Icelandic delicacy made from the meat of what animal?

ROCKEFELLER CENTER

Rockefeller Center was named after John D. Rockefeller Jr. (no surprise there), who leased the space from Columbia University in 1928. John D. originally planned to put together a financing syndicate and build a complex that included an opera house for the Metropolitan Opera. But he had bad timing. After the stock market crashed in 1929, he was forced to go it alone. Even the opera was reluctant to get on board.

Fortunately, with a name like Rockefeller you have very deep pockets. John D. renegotiated his line of credit and built twelve Art Deco buildings that eventually made him even more fabulously wealthy than he already was.

Subsequent owners were not always so lucky. The Mitsubishi Estate Company, which bought a majority share of the complex in 1989, filed for bankruptcy in 1995. Rock Center is now owned by Tishman Speyer Properties, one of the handful of huge private companies that own just about all the big buildings in the world.

Ben's Double or Nothing Bonus

Welcome to CSI: Cash Cab. *From a Latin word meaning "before the forum," what word means the science of crime scene investigation?*

AND THE ANSWERS ARE . . .

$50 questions

1. Pride
2. Laugh track
3. Cigars
4. Pop Rocks
5. Camels
6. Sulfur
7. Manifesto

Red Light Challenge 1

Aida
Beauty and the Beast
The Lion King
The Little Mermaid
Mary Poppins
Tarzan

8. Forbidden City
9. Prosecutions
10. Annie Oakley

$100 questions

1. Vacuum the floor
2. Istanbul (which used to be Constantinople)
3. Soy
4. Koala
5. Dudley Do-Right
6. Zero

7. Lumberjill
8. Mimosa
9. (Peter Carl) Fabergé
10. Dominoes

Red Light Challenge 2

Afghanistan
Kazakhstan
Kyrgyzstan
Pakistan
Tajikistan
Turkmenistan
Uzbekistan

$200 questions

1. (Ernest) Hemingway (technically, the cats
   are polydactyl)
2. Tarmac
3. Denouement
4. Sacagawea
5. The Champagne Room
6. Carl Jung

Red Light Challenge 3

A&W (All-American Foods)
KFC (Kentucky Fried Chicken)
Long John Silver's
Pizza Hut
Taco Bell
WingStreet

7. London
8. Echo
9. Lorax
10. Shark

Ben's Double or Nothing Bonus

Forensics

34TH STREET AND TENTH AVENUE TO PARK AVENUE AND 52ND STREET

(25 BLOCKS)

These questions are worth $50 each.

1. Also known as Gallows, what macabre grade-school game involves the drawing of an ill-fated stick figure?
2. Before setting her sights on sex education, what diminutive doctor served as a sniper in the Israeli Defense Force?
3. Coined by an AP reporter, what two-word term refers to the drought-stricken American plains of the 1930s?
4. Owned by a consortium of bog farmers, Ocean Spray is a leading producer of what tart edibles?
5. Famously performed by Michael Jackson, what dance move is believed to be based on the pantomime of French actor Jean-Louis Barrault?

THE EMPIRE STATE BUILDING

This trip passes right by the Empire State Building on 34th Street. A rarity in the construction business, the Empire State Building was finished under budget and ahead of schedule. How in the world did that happen?

The builders, Starrett Bros. & Eken, were, quite simply, startlingly efficient. They started by planning the work of the sixty trades involved in overlapping schedules, so that different parts of the building could be worked on at the same time. Then they built a system of supply carts on rails, pushed by people who, since this was during the Depression (construction started in 1929), were happy to spend their day pushing around carts loaded with hundreds of pounds of building materials. Instead of having the 10 million bricks needed for construction dumped in the nearby streets—which was how it was done in those days—they had trucks dump the bricks down a chute that led to a hopper in the basement. The bricks were then dropped into carts that were hoisted up to the appropriate floor.

Parts of the building were prefabricated off-site—that's a common construction technique now, but "prefab" wasn't even a word then.

The building's façade incorporated the 6,500 windows right into the outer wall, simplifying the work and using a lot less stone. This design meant they could put up the façade at a speedy rate of one story a day. In September 1930, the workers completed fourteen floors in ten days.

Electricians and plumbers began their work inside while the outside was still being completed. So the whole building was finished in one year and forty-five days. In a city where it takes a year to replace the escalator in a subway station, that's truly amazing.

These questions are worth $100 each.

1. In the game of croquet, wooden mallets tap wooden balls through what nonwooden hoops?
2. Treated with milk thistle by the ancient Greeks, cirrhosis is a chronic condition characterized by the scarring of what organ?
3. In what New Testament parable of forgiveness does a father welcome back his wayward, wasteful child?
4. What is Prince Charles of Great Britain's actual last name?
5. Feared by firefighters, what explosive phenomenon occurs when an oxygen-starved fire suddenly gets a breath of fresh air?

RED LIGHT CHALLENGE 1

Remember, this is worth $250 and you've got 30 seconds.

In the Caribbean, only five independent nations have populations that exceed one million. Name these five island nations.

These questions are worth $200 each.

1. In chemistry, what is the term for elements with the same atomic number but a different mass, such as carbon-12 and carbon-14?
2. An important player in the Middle East, what is the only nation in the world named after its current royal family?
3. Ordered by General Robert E. Lee, Pickett's Charge was a disastrous assault that took place during what Civil War battle?

RED LIGHT CHALLENGE 2

Crosstown rides always hit more red lights. The American Kennel Club divides its registered breeds into seven groups, plus the Miscellaneous Class. Name five of these seven canine categories.

4. Who did Muhammad Ali fight in the famous "Rumble in the Jungle"?
5. Sometimes referred to as "horse," what addictive drug was once sold by Bayer as a cough treatment?

Ben's Double or Nothing Bonus

When feasible, this finicky North American feline preys almost exclusively on the snowshoe hare. Slightly larger than a bobcat with tufts of hair on the tips of its ears, what is the name of this cold-weather predator?

AND THE ANSWERS ARE...

$50 questions

1. Hangman
2. Dr. Ruth Westheimer
3. Dust Bowl
4. Cranberries
5. Moonwalk

$100 questions

1. Wickets
2. Liver
3. The Prodigal Son
4. Windsor
5. Backdraft

Red Light Challenge 1

Cuba
Dominican Republic
Haiti
Jamaica
Trinidad and Tobago (either Trinidad or Tobago
alone are also okay)

$200 questions

1. Isotope
2. Saudi Arabia
3. Gettysburg

Red Light Challenge 2

Sporting
Hound
Working
Terrier
Toy
Nonsporting
Herding

4. George Foreman
5. Heroin

Ben's Double or Nothing Bonus

Lynx

WEST 14TH AND NINTH AVENUE
TO LEXINGTON AND 28TH STREET
(21 BLOCKS)

These questions are worth $50 each.

1. Name the U.S. state that captivates the imagination (and the appetite) with its slogan, "Great potatoes, tasty destinations."
2. What famously birthmarked politician led the Soviet Union from 1985 to 1991?
3. According to John Gray's bestselling relationship guide, men are from Mars and women are from where?
4. When performing the butterfly stroke, swimmers use a kick technique named after what marine mammal?

RED LIGHT CHALLENGE 1

Ben captains his cab alone, but seven crew members were ranking officers throughout the run of the original Star Trek *series. Name five of these seven enterprising characters. (Just the last names will be enough.) You have 30 seconds.*

These questions are worth $100 each.

1. What cut of steak is split right down the middle, with strip loin on one side and tenderloin on the other?
2. What purveyor of diet pills, abbreviated as "HLF" on the New York Stock Exchange, is credited with pioneering the modern infomercial?
3. Wi-fi, which establishes a cable-free connection to the Internet, is an abbreviation for what two-word phrase?
4. Lying low in L.A., a nearly intact mammoth skeleton was discovered in 2009 next to what famously sticky site?

BEN'S FAVORITE NEW YORK MUSEUMS

These are the ones the tourists don't go to.

Skyscraper Museum

You've got to love a museum that describes New York as "the world's first and foremost vertical metropolis." The museum is tucked into Battery Park City, which is worth a visit all by itself.

Museum of Sex

Yes, there are handcuffs and risqué photos and homemade sex machines, but there are also giant plush animals and sex toys with artfully aesthetic designs.

NYC Police Museum

Like the Museum of Sex, you will find handcuffs here. Also a visual record of how uniforms, guns, and nightsticks have changed through the ages, and police precinct ledgers dating from pivotal historical moments.

The Museum of the Moving Image

This is in Astoria, Queens, in what used to be the Kaufman Astoria Studios. That's where they shot the great Marx Brothers classics *The Cocoanuts* and *Animal Crackers*. I just think it's cool to have a museum dedicated to TV and the movies.

Fraunces Tavern

A museum that's also a bar—need I say more? This is where George Washington bid a tearful farewell to his officers in 1783, just nine days after they kicked the last of the British out of New York and the Revolution was over. The museum's collection includes a lock of Washington's hair and one of his false teeth, plus a lot of material about New York in the Colonial era. Study up and you'll do a lot better in *Cash Cab*.

These questions are worth $200 each.

1. What family of Venetian painters shares its last name with a champagne cocktail?
2. Although it's an amphibian, what animal's name comes from a Greek word meaning "fire lizard"?
3. What style of Australian sheepskin boots did Paris Hilton help popularize?
4. Containing sections of the Torah, what small box do Jewish households often affix to their doorframe?

RED LIGHT CHALLENGE 2

Another red light, another Red Light Challenge. This is worth $250.

Barack Obama has fifteen positions in his presidential cabinet. George Washington had only four. Name three of those four original cabinet positions.

Ben's Double or Nothing Bonus

Around 1200 B.C.E., this archaeological site was the home of a prophesying priestess named Pythia. Referenced by everyone from Aristotle to Xeno, this authoritative oracle was the major attraction in what Greek town?

$50 questions

1. Idaho
2. (Mikhail) Gorbachev
3. Venus
4. Dolphin

Red Light Challenge 1

Captain James T. Kirk
First Officer Mr. Spock
Ship's Doctor Leonard "Bones" McCoy
Lieutenant Nyota Uhura (Does anyone even
    remember the episode where they told you
    her first name?)
Chief Engineer Montgomery "Scotty" Scott
Ensign Hikaru Sulu
Ensign Pavel Chekov

$100 questions

1. T-bone
2. Herbalife
3. Wireless fidelity
4. La Brea Tar Pits

$200 questions

1. Bellini
2. Salamander
3. UGG
4. Mezuzah

. . . AND THE ANSWERS ARE

Red Light Challenge 2

Secretary of State
Secretary of the Treasury
Secretary of War
Attorney General

Ben's Double or Nothing Bonus

Delphi

FIFTH AVENUE AND 45TH
TO WALL STREET
(70 BLOCKS)

These questions are worth $50 each.

1. 1980's "Miracle on Ice" refers to the U.S. gold medal in what sport?
2. What famous motor home brand took its name from a tribe of Native Americans in Nebraska?
3. According to Oxford's *Dictionary of Slang*, what does a "five finger discount" refer to?
4. Popular for its cosmetic use, what toxin paralyzes the muscles that cause wrinkles?
5. What was the first U.S. state to make same-sex marriages legal?
6. Ben drives the most trusted cab in New York, but what TV network bills itself as "The most trusted name in news"?

RED LIGHT CHALLENGE 1

We're stopped at a red light, so it's time for a Red Light Challenge. Remember, this is worth $250 and you have 30 seconds.

In addition to bratwurst and the Autobahn, Germany has some world-class cities. As of 2011, what are four of the five most populous cities in Germany?

7. What Italian term that literally means "from the chapel" refers to singing with no musical accompaniment?

8. What parasitic plant, used to solicit kisses at Christmas, was once believed to cure epilepsy?

These questions are worth $100 each.

1. What large African mammal comes in fun varieties like Somali, Smoky, and Nubian?

2. Henry Moore and Auguste Rodin are most associated with what art form?

3. What statistic, abbreviated CPI, is used by the federal government to track the cost of living in the United States?

WALL STREET

Yes, there really was a wall on Wall Street. It was made of logs twelve to thirteen feet high, with sharp points hewn at the top. The Dutch built it in 1653, when Oliver Cromwell, the same guy who overthrew the king back in Britain, declared war on the Dutch Republic.

All of that happened over in Europe, but somehow the citizens of the Dutch colony of New Amsterdam thought the British settlements all the way up in New Haven, Connecticut (several days' gallop away), might be a threat. So they put up a wall across the northern edge of their city, from the Hudson to the East River. There was a gate at what is today Broadway and a water gate at Pearl Street (which was the shoreline at the time).

Cromwell got sick and died in 1658. The British monarchy was reestablished, and in 1661, in an amazing display of belated revenge, the restored king, Charles II, had Cromwell's body dug up so he could execute him.

King Charles presided over the Great Plague in London, which was followed by the Great Fire. He also presided over the British capture of New Amsterdam. The Brits came by sea and avoided the wall entirely. Charles renamed the city after his brother, the famous Duke of York. The new British governor tore down the wall. And then there was nothing to stop the rich people from moving uptown.

4. In addition to its famous jewelry and silverware, what company makes championship trophies for the NBA and the NFL?

5. Because its high sugar concentration kills most bacteria, what natural sweetener did the Assyrians use to embalm the dead?

6. What European capital lies on the banks of the Tiber River?
7. In 1912, the crew of the *Carpathia* helped assist the survivors of what nautical disaster?
8. Marked by a sudden spike in retail sales, Black Friday falls the day after which U.S. holiday?

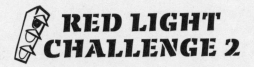

RED LIGHT CHALLENGE 2

Miss this one and you might need to find a cheaper ride. Name four of the six cities with the world's busiest subway systems.

These questions are worth $200 each.

1. Greek for "many gods," what word describes a belief in multiple deities?
2. In 1961, what Russian made history by becoming the first human to travel into space?
3. Doctors put a vest made of what elemental metal on patients to shield them from X-ray radiation?
4. Not including overtime periods, how long is a regulation World Cup soccer game?

RED LIGHT CHALLENGE 3

Unlike the Cash Cab, which crawls along in New York traffic, some animals reach speeds of up to fifty miles per hour. Name four of the five fastest animals on land.

5. For thirty-two years, Helen Gurley Brown was editor-in-chief of what fashion magazine?
6. More coveted than a Purple Heart, what is the highest military decoration in our armed forces?
7. The human nose contains what dense connective tissue that lacks blood vessels or nerves?
8. Marvel Comics is one of the two largest comic book companies in the United States. Name the other one.

HIGH-DENSITY TAXI TOWNS

Just seven metropolitan areas account for 36 percent of all the taxi and limo drivers in the United States. New York, of course, leads the top seven with more than 40,000 drivers. Chicago, Los Angeles, Washington, D.C., San Francisco, Las Vegas, and Boston round out the group. New York has 4.6 taxi and limo drivers per one thousand people, making it the highest-density taxi town in America.

Ben's Double or Nothing Bonus

Ponte Vecchio (it means "old bridge") was one of the lucky landmarks spared by the Germans in World War II. Currently bombarded by tourists, this steadfast structure spans the Arno River in what European city?

AND THE ANSWERS ARE . . .

$100 questions

1. Giraffe
2. Sculpture
3. Consumer Price Index
4. Tiffany's
5. Honey
6. Rome
7. The sinking of the *Titanic*
8. Thanksgiving

Red Light Challenge 1

Berlin
Hamburg
Munich (München)
Cologne (Köln)
Frankfurt

7. A cappella
8. Mistletoe

$50 questions

1. Ice hockey
2. Winnebago
3. Shoplifting
4. Botox
5. Massachusetts
6. CNN

Red Light Challenge 2

Moscow
Tokyo
Seoul
Mexico City
New York City
Paris

$200 questions

1. Polytheism
2. Yuri Gagarin
3. Lead
4. 90 minutes

Red Light Challenge 3

Cheetah
Antelope
Wildebeest (or Gnu)
Lion
Gazelle

5. *Cosmopolitan*
6. Medal of Honor
7. Cartilage
8. DC Comics

Ben's Double or Nothing Bonus

Florence, Italy (And they're not kidding when
they say old—it was built in 1345.)

42ND STREET AND FIFTH AVENUE

TO 71ST AND SECOND

(35 BLOCKS)

These questions are worth $50 each.

1. When shaken too violently, pinball machines traditionally flash what four-letter word?
2. What brand once advertised its product with the famous slogan "plop plop fizz fizz"?
3. Ranging from 0 to 24, what unit of measure reveals the proportion of pure gold in a metal alloy?
4. In the Book of Revelation, what group of equestrians represents War, Famine, Pestilence, and Death?
5. Better than a Pocket Fisherman, what Native American tool traditionally features an ax at one end and a pipe at the other?

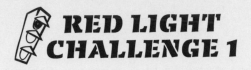

RED LIGHT CHALLENGE 1

You knew a Snow White's Dwarfs question would eventually pop up, and here it is. Snow White hung out with seven famous dwarfs, none of them named Cabbie. What were their names? You have 30 seconds to come up with all seven.

These questions are worth $100 each.

1. What gorilla, taught by Dr. Penny Patterson, knows more than 1,000 words in sign language?
2. In 1968, Johnny Cash recorded a live concert album at what California state prison?
3. Meaning "fire bowl" in Japanese, what term refers to a small, charcoal-burning grilling station?
4. When served as dinner, deer meat can be rather chewy. What is this gamey meat called?
5. In the automotive world, what is BMW an abbreviation for?

YELLOW CABS

John D. Hertz started out as a car salesman and ended up with the biggest rental car agency in the United States. But while Hertz Rent-A-Car once claimed their only desire was to put you in the driver's seat, John D.'s first business was based on keeping you out of the driver's seat: He founded the Yellow Cab Company in Chicago in 1915. In those days, fleet owners typically manufactured their own cars as well as hiring drivers. Hertz decided to paint his cabs yellow after he read a University of Chicago study that said yellow was the most visible color at greater distances. Clearly, Hertz was a visionary.

Hertz's distinctive yellow cabs became popular in the Windy City and were quickly franchised throughout the United States, including New York. In the early 1920s, Yellow Cab was locked in a bitter rivalry with Checker Cab, which led to a number of shootings and firebombings—including a firebombing of Hertz's horse-racing stables.

Meanwhile, in 1924 Hertz acquired a little rental car business and renamed it Hertz Drive-Ur-Self Corporation. In 1926, he sold a majority share in the taxi and rental car business to General Motors. Then, in 1953, he bought back the rental business from GM. GM unloaded the cab business in 1996 to a group headed by a former New York City cabby. Hertz kept the rental company this time and made a fortune helping people avoid cab rides.

These questions are worth $200 each.

1. In the Jewish faith, a mohel is a professional who performs what ritual?
2. Earning about sixty million bucks a month

trafficking drugs, Pablo Escobar was the kingpin of what Colombian cartel?

3. With a name meaning "swift thief," what predatory dinosaur slashed its prey using sickle-shaped claws?

RED LIGHT CHALLENGE 2

English, German, and French are the three most commonly spoken languages in the European Union. Name six of the other seven that make up the top ten.
This is worth $250.

4. In 1952, Richard Nixon played upon voter sympathy by mentioning his dog in a speech. Name this famous canine.

5. What infamous Missouri bank robber was killed by a member of his own gang for a $10,000 reward?

Ben's Double or Nothing Bonus

At an Islamic mosque, the faithful are traditionally called to prayer five times a day from the top of a tower. Meaning "lighthouse" in Arabic, what is the term for this soaring spire?

$50 questions

1. Tilt
2. Alka-Seltzer
3. Karat
4. The Four Horsemen of the Apocalypse
5. Tomahawk

Red Light Challenge 1

Bashful
Doc
Dopey
Grumpy
Happy
Sleepy
Sneezy

$100 questions

1. Koko
2. Folsom (State Prison)
3. Hibachi
4. Venison
5. Bavarian Motor Works

$200 questions

1. Circumcision
2. Medellín
3. Velociraptor

AND THE ANSWERS ARE . . .

Red Light Challenge 2

Italian
Spanish
Polish
Dutch
Greek
Czech
Swedish

4. Checkers
5. Jesse James

Ben's Double or Nothing Bonus

Minaret

BROADWAY AND 49TH STREET
TO COLUMBUS AVENUE AND 91ST
(41 BLOCKS)

These questions are worth $50 each.

1. Obsession and Eternity are both brands of what?
2. In New York, a gathering of taxis is called rush hour. In nature, a gathering of what is called a "gaggle"?
3. What spicy sauce is produced on Avery Island in Louisiana and is sold in more than one hundred sixty countries?
4. What mogul put the T in cable network TBS?
5. Completed in 1970, the Aswan High Dam required the relocation of more than ninety thousand residents who lived along the banks of what river?
6. With measurements of 19-19-19, what is the name of Popeye the Sailor's gangly gal pal?

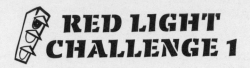

RED LIGHT CHALLENGE 1

We're stopped at a red light, so it's time for a Red Light Challenge. Remember, this is worth $250.

Seven elements from the Periodic Table are traded on the New York Mercantile Exchange. Name five of these seven highly valued commodities. You have 30 seconds.

These questions are worth $100 each.

1. Members of what organization are sometimes referred to as "Friends of Bill W."?
2. Often served with sushi, what root is an effective treatment for nausea?
3. What is the nickname of Interstate 495, which forms a sixty-four-mile circle around Washington, D.C.?
4. Translated as "driving pleasure," what peculiar German word did Volkswagen introduce to American consumers?
5. When John Hancock put his John Hancock on the Declaration of Independence, he wrote not on paper but on what?
6. What northwestern state pays homage to rodentia with its nickname "The Beaver State"?

BROADWAY

If you get in a cab on Broadway with plenty of cash, the driver can take you all the way to Albany. You can play a lot of *Cash Cab* on a trip that long.

Broadway, probably the oldest highway in America, begins just above Bowling Green and, although its name changes in Westchester, goes all the way to New York's state capital. It began as the Wickquasgeck Trail, which the locals hacked out along the length of Manhattan. When the Dutch moved in, they renamed it Breedeweg, which means . . . broad way. It was broad because part of it led from the entrance of the city fort up to the gate at Wall Street. The street was extra wide near the fort so the soldiers had room to drill.

When New Amsterdam changed its name to New York, the street changed its name to Broadway. It remained broad. Also crooked.

In 1811, the city imposed a strict grid plan on New York's streets. That's why it's so easy to get around today. But because Broadway was a well-established north-south road more than one hundred years before, the bureaucrats left it alone (showing a rare respect for history). Broadway crosses our little island diagonally, and as a result, odd slivers of real estate turn up where it meets with other north-south avenues. That's one reason why so many "squares" in New York are actually triangles.

Broadway runs the entire length of Manhattan, north to Inwood. The Broadway Bridge then spans Spuyten Duyvil Creek and Broadway runs all the way up to Westchester, where it turns into the Albany Post Road, now known as U.S. Route 9. The Albany Post Road connects New York City and Albany, and was used for . . . delivering post, a.k.a. the mail.

Back in 1880, Broadway was one of the first streets in the United States to be lit by electric lights. It was so bright compared to the gaslights everywhere else that it was nicknamed The Great White Way.

These questions are worth $200 each.

1. What is the term for the group of electors who lock themselves in a room to choose a new Pope?
2. What specific branch of physics describes the properties of light and how it reacts with matter?

RED LIGHT CHALLENGE 2

Eight nations use a form of currency called the peso. For 250 pesos, name five of these eight countries.

3. Just west of Colorado Springs, what famous mountain is the site of a notoriously treacherous annual auto race?
4. Similar to a jellyfish, what poisonous sea creature was named for a type of battleship?
5. Tchaikovsky was the featured conductor at the 1891 opening of what Manhattan classical music venue?
6. Despite public outcry, Pluto was demoted in 2006 and is now known as what type of heavenly body?

NEW YORK CAB FARES

How do cab fares in New York stack up against the rest of the country? They're eleventh highest among the big metro areas. The average New York fare is $9.61 for a 2.8 mile trip, or $11.44 when surcharges and tips are added in.

Ben's Double or Nothing Bonus

Derived from an old French word meaning "wheel," roulette is popular from Las Vegas to Monaco. On a standard casino roulette wheel, what is the only number that appears on a green background?

AND THE ANSWERS ARE . . .

$50 questions

1. Colognes
2. Geese
3. Tabasco
4. Ted Turner
5. Nile
6. Olive Oyl

Red Light Challenge 1

Aluminum
Copper
Gold
Palladium
Platinum
Silver
Uranium

$100 questions

1. Alcoholics Anonymous
2. Ginger
3. The Beltway
4. Fahrvergnügen (no need to spell it!)
5. Parchment
6. Oregon

$200 questions

1. Conclave
2. Optics

Red Light Challenge 2

Argentina
Chile
Colombia
Cuba
Dominican Republic
Mexico
Philippines
Uruguay

3. Pike's Peak
4. Man o' War
5. Carnegie Hall
6. Dwarf planet

Ben's Double or Nothing Bonus

Zero

E 33rd St
E 32nd St
E 31st St
E 30th St
W 29th St
W 28th St
E 29th St
E 28th St
W 27th St
W 25th St
Madison Square Park
E 26th St
E 25th St
E 24th St
W 24th St
Chelsea Waterside
W 23rd St
W 22nd St
W 21st St
W 20th St
E 23rd St
E 22nd St
E 21st St
Gramercy Park
E 20th St
W 19th St
W 18th St
W 17th St
W 16th St
W 15th St
E 19th St
E 18th St
E 17th St
Union Square
E 15th St
Stuyvesant Square
W 14th St
E 14th St
W 13th St
E 13th St
W 12th St
W 11th St
W 10th St
E 12th St
E 11th St
E 10th St
E 9th St
E 8th St
E 7th St
E 6th St
E 5th St
E 4th St
E 3rd St
E 2nd St
E 1st St
St Marks Pl
Tompkins Square Park
10th Ave
9th Ave
8th Ave
7th Ave
7th Ave S
6th Ave
5th Ave
Avenue Of The Americas
Broadway
Park Ave S
Lexington Ave
Irving Pl
University Pl
4th Ave
3rd Ave
2nd Ave
1st Ave
Avenue A
Avenue B
Avenue C
E River Dr
Marginal St
Washington St
Hudson St
Bank St
Perry St
Christopher
Morton St
Clarkson St
Bleecker St
W 3rd St
MacDougal St
Mercer St
Lafayette St
Bowery
E Houston St
Stanton St
Rivington St
Loisaida Ave
Pitt St
Prince St
Spring St
Elizabeth St
Chrystie St
Avenue Of The Immigrants
Ludlow St
Essex St
Allen St
Broome St
Grand St
Canal St
Walker St
Hester St
Mulberry St
Mott St
Baxter St
Eldridge St
Varick St
W Broadway
Greene St
Laight St
Beach St
White St
Leonard St
Worth St
Duane St
Thomas Paine Park
Centre St
Chambers St
Warren St
Murray St
Vesey St
Church St
City Hall Park
Park Row
Frankfort St
Ann St
Catherine St
Market St
Madison St
Cherry St
E Broadway
Henry St
Seward Park
E River Piers
Franklin D Roosevelt Dr
Manhattan Brg
Brooklyn Brg
West St
N River Piers
Greenwich St
N End Ave
Governor Nelson A Rockefeller Park
North Cove
Liberty St
Albany St
Nassau St
William St
Pearl St
Front St
South St
9
278

122ND STREET AND WEST END AVENUE

TO MADISON AND 94TH

(32 BLOCKS)

These questions are worth $50 each.

1. Herpetology is the study of reptiles and what other classification of animals?
2. What aquatic sport merges elements of ballet and gymnastics, and became an official Olympic event in 1984?

RED LIGHT CHALLENGE 1

This Red Light Challenge tests your knowledge of a local libation. Name four of the five types of alcohol that are mixed to make a Long Island Iced Tea. You have 30 seconds and you can win $250—enough to buy plenty of cocktails.

3. What ethical principle of Buddhism states that all actions have a consequence?

4. In the song "Take Me Out to the Ballgame," a request is made for peanuts and what other classic snack food?

GRANT'S TOMB

It's the classic New York joke: Who's buried in Grant's Tomb? The answer is nobody.

Ulysses S. Grant and his wife, Julia, are entombed in the mausoleum at 122nd Street and Riverside Drive. But they're both aboveground.

These questions are worth $100 each.

1. The studio Dreamworks SKG was founded by three Hollywood bigwigs. Who put the G in SKG?

2. Meaning "fox" in Spanish, by what name is swashbuckler Don Diego de la Vega better known?

3. Abbreviated "VC," what outside source of equity is commonly used to finance high-risk, high-tech start-ups?

4. What New York rapper and entrepreneur became a part owner of the New Jersey Nets basketball team in 2004?

RED LIGHT CHALLENGE 2

We're stopped at a red light, so it's time for another Red Light Challenge.

The so-called "urban triangle" of Texas contains five metropolitan areas, each with more than 200,000 people. Name all five of these metro areas.

These questions are worth $200 each.

1. In geology, what is the theory scientists use to explain the phenomenon of continental drift?

2. In 2005, Mark Felt finally admitted that he is what mysterious historical figure?

3. The inventor of a popular bidding system, writer Charles Goren made revolutionary contributions to what four-person card game?

4. What Asian nation conducted its first nuclear test explosion in 1974 under the code name "Smiling Buddha"?

WHAT HAPPENED IN 1899?

Eighteen ninety-nine was a year of records for taxis and for American car culture in general. On May 20, New York taxi driver Jacob German received the first speeding ticket in the United States. And on September 13, a sixty-eight-year-old man named Henry H. Bliss was helping a friend get off a New York streetcar when an electric-powered taxi swerved and hit him. Bliss became the first American to die in an automobile accident.

Ben's Double or Nothing Bonus

From Julia Child to Chef Boyardee, serious cooks favor a white, pleated hat that stands as tall as a soufflé. Taken from French, what is the term for this traditional culinary headgear?

AND THE ANSWERS ARE . . .

$50 questions

1. Amphibians
2. Synchronized swimming

Red Light Challenge 1

Vodka
Tequila
Rum
Gin
Triple sec
3. Karma
4. Cracker Jack

$100 questions

1. (David) Geffen
2. Zorro
3. Venture capital
4. Jay-Z

Red Light Challenge 2

Austin
San Antonio
Houston
Dallas–Fort Worth
Waco

$200 questions

1. Plate tectonics
2. Deep Throat
3. (Contract) Bridge
4. India

Ben's Double or Nothing Bonus

Toque

HOUSTON AND BOWERY
TO EIGHTH AVENUE AND 55TH STREET
(61 BLOCKS)

These questions are worth $50 each.

1. A Spanish galleon, the space shuttle, and two palm trees adorn the commemorative quarter of what U.S. state?

2. Defined as "a Web-based audio broadcast," what Internet term was inspired by Apple's ubiquitous MP3 player?

3. In an unhappy coincidence, the movie *The China Syndrome,* about the cover-up of safety problems at a nuclear power plant, opened two weeks before an infamous accident at what facility?

4. In 2005, the European Union officially designated what Greek cheese as 70 percent sheep's milk and 30 percent goat's milk?

5. In 1996, a member of the NHL champion Colorado Avalanche had his daughter baptized in what storied trophy?

6. Bowhead and beluga are both species of what mammal?

RED LIGHT CHALLENGE 1

Red light ahead, so it's time for a Red Light Challenge. Remember, this is worth $250.

Five last names have been shared by more than one U.S. president. Name four of these presidential surnames. You have 30 seconds.

7. Resembling an eighteen-story golf ball, Spaceship Earth is an architectural icon of what Disney World theme park?

INTERIOR ROOM

Currently, the Ford Crown Victoria and the Toyota Sienna are the two most common New York cab models. Which is roomier? Depends on whether you need to stretch your legs or your neck. The Crown Victoria has more leg room (45.6 inches, versus 39.6 inches for the Sienna), but the Toyota has 40.2 inches of headroom compared to the Ford's 37.9 inches.

8. Originally named "Pretzel," what iconic Hasbro game is not recommended for the clumsy or the color blind?

These questions are worth $100 each.

1. What iconic guitarist, named for composer Jerome Kern, lost half a finger in a childhood incident with an ax?
2. An oceanographer at Florida State, Dr. Doron Nof, theorizes that extreme wind may have caused what book of Exodus miracle?
3. What adjectival form is more extreme than the comparative, and is exemplified in the phrase "the best and the brightest"?
4. Two octaves below an oboe, what large double reed instrument was used in pop recordings before the advent of the electric drum?

RED LIGHT CHALLENGE 2

The University of California has ten campuses, including UC Davis and UC Merced. Let's C if U can name five of the remaining eight campuses.

BEN'S FAVORITE NEW YORK TAXI MOVIES

Taxi (1932) starred James Cagney as cabbie Matt Nolan, an Irishman who happens to speak Yiddish (because the movie does take place in New York, after all). The Consolidated Cab Company tries to run all the independent taxi drivers out of business, and Nolan wants to make things right. In the process, he learns that brains beat brawn and also says the now-famous line, "Come out and take it, you dirty, yellow-bellied rat, or I'll give it to you through the door!"

Taxi Driver (1976), directed by Martin Scorsese and starring Robert DeNiro, is a classic for so many reasons. Jodie Foster's portrayal of a twelve-year-old prostitute made her a very famous little girl. DeNiro asks the immortal rhetorical question, "You lookin' at me?" And Travis Bickle takes Betsy (Cybill Shepherd) on the worst first date of all time—to a Swedish sex flick in Times Square. That was the old Times Square, before it became Disneyland.

Night on Earth (1991), directed by Jim Jarmusch, tells the stories of five taxi drivers around the world and their passengers. It starts in Los Angeles, where a driver picks up a talent agent who offers her an acting job; the driver proceeds to explain why driving a cab is way more interesting than acting. Next is New York, where an immigrant cabdriver (imagine that!) gets a lesson in New York geography, culture, and slang from Giancarlo Esposito and Rosie Perez. In Paris, a blind girl is picked up by a cabdriver from the Ivory Coast and teaches him a thing or two about being independent. In Rome, Roberto Benigni plays perhaps the funniest taxi driver ever (possibly even funnier than me) as he picks up an ailing priest and pretty much talks him to death. And then in Helsinki an industrial worker gets laid off and he and his drunk friends have a contest with their cabdriver to see who can be more depressed.

5. In European folklore, what is the term for a supernatural child who has been secretly swapped with a normal one?
6. Signifying purity in the Shinto religion, salt is traditionally thrown into the ring at the beginning of what contact sport?
7. Said to taste like pork, what Southwestern species of roadkill was called the "poverty pig" during the Great Depression?
8. What giant member of the grass family grows up to four feet a day and is often used to make sustainable wood floors?

These questions are worth $200 each.

1. The geographical term "America" is derived from the first name of what sixteenth-century Italian explorer?
2. A popular option on digital cameras, what variety of single-color photograph uses shades of brown instead of gray?

RED LIGHT CHALLENGE 3

This Red Light Challenge tosses you on the high seas. In terms of mass, name five of the eight most abundant chemical elements found in ocean water.

3. Though he bested both Hitler and the Red Menace, what patriotic Marvel superhero was taken down by a sniper in 2007?

4. In a standard game of bowling, how many strikes in a row would a bowler have to throw to achieve a perfect score of three hundred?

5. A pioneer in the field of special-effects makeup, what silent film actor was known as "The Man of a Thousand Faces"?

6. What epic poem, known for its graphic violence, begins, "Sing, goddess, of the wrath of Achilles"?

7. A type of technology used to propel trains without using wheels, "maglev" is short for what two words?

8. Ironically manufactured by prison inmates, New Hampshire's license plates are emblazoned with what state motto?

Ben's Double or Nothing Bonus

During the nine-hunded-day siege of Leningrad during World War II, employees of this famous St. Petersburg museum had to eat furniture glue to survive. What is the name of this enduring Russian institution?

AND THE ANSWERS ARE . . .

$50 questions

1. Florida
2. Podcast (inspired by the iPod)
3. Three Mile Island
4. Feta
5. Stanley Cup
6. Whale

Red Light Challenge 1

Adams
Bush
Harrison
Johnson
Roosevelt

7. EPCOT Center
8. Twister

$100 questions

1. Jerry Garcia
2. Parting of the Red Sea
3. Superlative
4. Bassoon

Red Light Challenge 2

Berkeley
Irvine
Los Angeles
Riverside

San Diego
San Francisco
Santa Barbara
Santa Cruz

5. Changeling
6. Sumo wrestling
7. Armadillo
8. Bamboo

$200 questions

1. Amerigo Vespucci
2. Sepia (tone)

Red Light Challenge 3

Oxygen
Hydrogen
Chlorine
Sodium
Magnesium
Sulfur
Calcium
Potassium

3. Captain America
4. 12
5. Lon Chaney (Sr.)
6. *Iliad*
7. Magnetic levitation
8. Live Free or Die

Ben's Double or Nothing Bonus

The Hermitage

CARNEGIE HALL
TO 84TH AND COLUMBUS
(28 BLOCKS)

These questions are worth $50 each.

1. An arachnophobe's nightmare, what large, furry spider was originally named for an Italian city?

2. In *Superman*, Clark Kent was a reporter for what major metropolitan newspaper?

3. Patented by its inventor around 1900, what type of bed folds out of the wall?

4. In 2007, what grandmother of six became the first female Speaker of the U.S. House of Representatives?

5. Just as *Cash Cab* is the un-game show, what soft drink once billed itself as the "un-cola"?

CARNEGIE HALL

How do you get to Carnegie Hall? Practice. Or you can take a cab to Seventh Avenue and 57th Street.

Carnegie is one of those remarkable old concert halls that were built before the science of acoustics was invented (which was also before microphones were invented) and that therefore have perfect acoustics. At Carnegie, you can hear every note from every seat.

Because acoustic scientists don't really know what makes Carnegie's sound so great, when the hall was renovated in 1983 they weren't sure whether or not to fix a big hole cut in the ceiling back in 1946. They went ahead and fixed it. And then, musicians said, the sound resonating off the stage floor went dead.

The Carnegie bosses and the renovation architects denied it, and told everyone to stop whining. They even brought in an acoustician, who stuck various objects on the ceiling in an effort to improve the sound. But the critics kept complaining. They said it sounded as if there was a big slab of concrete under the stage reflecting all the sound out in a harsh way, instead of gently resonating it.

Then in the early 1990s the stage floor began to warp. Finally, workers tore it up to look for the problem and found—a big slab of concrete. The architectural firm that did the renovation could not figure out how it got there (how does a slab of concrete end up anywhere without someone noticing?). But they took it out, restored the stage floor, and now the sound is perfect again.

These questions are worth $100 each.

1. Borrowed from Kurt Weill's *The Threepenny Opera*, what Bobby Darin hit begins with the line, "Oh, the shark has pretty teeth, dear"?
2. Harlan, the portly, bespectacled founder of Kentucky Fried Chicken, is better known as who?
3. How many goals must a hockey player put past the goalie to score a hat trick?

RED LIGHT CHALLENGE 1

As always, this Red Light Challenge is worth $250 and you have 30 seconds.

Eight U.S. states have two-letter postal abbreviations that end with the letter A. Name six of the eight states.

4. Designed by Mikhail Kalashnikov in 1947, what assault rifle is ominously featured on the flag of Mozambique?
5. What repetitive strain injury is often the result of too much typing or video-game playing?

These questions are worth $200 each.

1. Known as the godfather of grunge, what singer of "Harvest Moon" is a minority shareholder in the Lionel toy train company?
2. From an Old English word for "pulley," what mechanical winding device is designed to haul or hoist loads?

RED LIGHT CHALLENGE 2

In Shakespeare's Hamlet, *eight characters die during the course of the play. Name five of these eight unfortunate characters.*

3. Also known as "Montana tendergroin," the private parts of a bull are used to make a regional delicacy called Rocky Mountain what?
4. With more than 100 million registered users, what Internet phone company was snapped up by eBay in 2005?
5. Considered by Tolstoy to be his first true novel, what book finally became a bestseller in 2004 after it received a blessing from Oprah Winfrey?

Ben's Double or Nothing Bonus

In a marching band, the members who play this instrument have always marched to a different beat, especially with fifty pounds of brass wound around their bodies. Named for an American composer, what is this portable version of the tuba?

$50 questions

1. Tarantula (the city is Taranto)
2. *The Daily Planet*
3. Murphy bed
4. Nancy Pelosi
5. 7-Up

$100 questions

1. "Mack the Knife"
2. Colonel Sanders
3. Three

Red Light Challenge 1

California
Georgia
Iowa
Louisiana
Massachusetts
Pennsylvania
Virginia
Washington

4. AK-47
5. Carpal tunnel syndrome

$200 questions

1. Neil Young
2. Winch

... AND THE ANSWERS ARE

Red Light Challenge 2

Claudius
Gertrude ("Hamlet's mom" is not acceptable)
Guildenstern
Hamlet
Laertes
Ophelia
Polonius
Rosencrantz

3. Oysters
4. Skype
5. *Anna Karenina*

Ben's Double or Nothing Bonus

Sousaphone

E 33rd St
E 32nd St
E 31st St
E 30th St
W 29th St
W 28th St
E 28th St
E 29th St
W 27th St
5th Ave
Avenue Of The Americas
Park Ave S
Lexington Ave
E River Dr
Marginal St
W 25th St
Madison Square Park
E 26th St
W 24th St
Chelsea Waterside
W 23rd St
E 24th St
E 25th St
W 22nd St
E 23rd St
W 21st St
W 20th St
E 22nd St
E 21st St
E 23rd St
10th Ave
9th Ave
8th Ave
Broadway
W 19th St
Gramercy Park
E 20th St
E River Piers
Avenue C
W 18th St
W 17th St
5th Ave
E 19th St
E 18th St
E 17th St
W 16th St
W 15th St
Union Square
Irving Pl
Stuyvesant Square
7th Ave
W 14th St
E 15th St
E 14th St
1st Ave
E 14th St
E 15th St
10th Ave
Washington St
Hudson St
W 12th St
W 13th St
University Pl
E 10th St
4th Ave
3rd Ave
E 11th St
E 12th St
Avenue B
Avenue C
11th Ave
W 11th St
7th Ave S
6th Ave
5th Ave
E 10th St
E 9th St
E 8th St
Avenue A
Tompkins Square Park
E 8th St
Bank St
Perry St
W 10th St
MacDougal St
Mercer St
Lafayette St
St Marks Pl
E 7th St
E 6th St
Christopher St
W 3rd St
E 5th St
Bowery
2nd Ave
E 4th St
Loisaida Ave
E 3rd St
Morton St
7th Ave S
Bleecker St
E 2nd St
Clarkson St
Bleecker St
E 1st St
E Houston St
Varick St
6th Ave
W Broadway
Greene St
Broadway
Prince St
Elizabeth St
Chrystie St
Avenue Of The Immigrants
Stanton St
Rivington St
Ludlow St
Pitt St
Hudson St
Spring St
Avenue Of The Americas
Broome St
Mulberry St
Mott St
Allen St
Broome St
9
Grand St
Lafayette St
Bowery
Essex St
Grand St
E Broadway
Henry St
Canal St
Baxter St
Eldridge St
Laight St
Walker St
Hester St
Seward Park
Beach St
N River Piers
West St
Greenwich St
White St
Centre St
Madison St
W Broadway
Leonard St
Worth St
Cherry St
E River Piers
Duane St
Thomas Paine Park
Catherine St
Market St
Chambers St
Park Row
Governor Nelson A Rockefeller Park
N End Ave
Warren St
City Hall Park
Franklin D Roosevelt Dr
Manhattan Brg
Murray St
Church St
Frankfort St
Vesey St
Ann St
Pearl St
Brooklyn Brg
North Cove
Nassau St
William St
Liberty St
Pearl St
Front St
South St
Albany St
278
Esplanade

MADISON AND 87TH STREET
TO 125TH STREET AND SEVENTH AVENUE
(36 BLOCKS)

These questions are worth $50 each.

1. In the fascinating world of fractions, what is the term for the digit that appears above the denominator?
2. According to an Auburn University study, what simple style of sandal is even worse for your feet than high heels?
3. Named for an alloy of copper, what prehistoric period is sandwiched in between the Stone Age and the Iron Age?
4. In the Irish county of Tipperary, a 24/7 Webcam enables Internet users around the world to look for what supernatural creatures?
5. Home to an annual Trek Fest, Riverside, Iowa, claims to be the "official FUTURE birthplace" of what famous captain?

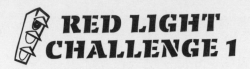

RED LIGHT CHALLENGE 1

Taxis are required to stop at all red lights, but that gives you a Red Light Challenge. Remember, this is worth $250. You have 30 seconds.

In the 2010 Global Fortune 500, seven oil and gas companies made it into the top twenty biggest companies in the world. Name five of these seven oil giants.

6. Now containing zero trans fats, what skinny variety of Girl Scout cookie accounts for 25 percent of annual sales?

TOURISTS AND TAXIS

Taxi drivers love tourists. Visitors to New York take about 38 million taxi trips a year, which averages 2.5 trips per overnight visitor. Hotel guests average one cab ride to or from their hotel each day. Plus, taxis are the number one way people get from Manhattan to New York's airports; 39 percent of people heading to the airport from Manhattan take a taxi.

These questions are worth $100 each.

1. In 1864, President Abraham Lincoln autographed copies of what iconic executive order to raise funds for wounded soldiers?

2. Meaning "ship" in Latin, what is the term for the area of a cathedral in which the congregation sits?

3. The mother of Track and Trig, in 2008 Sarah Palin welcomed a grandson named what?

4. Comparable to an English duke, what title was held by the chief magistrates of Venice for almost one thousand years?

5. Functioning as a prenatal shock absorber, what fluid protects a fetus from the knocks and pings of day-to-day life?

6. In the development stage, Scooby-Doo started out as a sheepdog to avoid confusion with what comic strip Great Dane?

RED LIGHT CHALLENGE 2

This Red Light Challenge takes us to our hockey-crazed neighbors to the north. Name five of the seven Canadian cities that are home to an NHL team.

These questions are worth $200 each.

1. Referring to its quiet rubber soles, what athletic shoe brand introduced the word "sneakers" in a 1917 ad campaign?
2. Sharing a name with his "terrible" grandson, which "great" ruler liberated Russia from the Mongol hordes?

THE APOLLO THEATER

The Apollo Theater, on West 125th Street, is one of those legendary places that opened back when everyone went uptown to Harlem to hear great music. What a lot of people don't remember is that Harlem clubs were often segregated, and the Apollo started out that way too—it opened in 1914 as a burlesque house for whites only.

But in 1934 it changed hands, and the new owner welcomed everyone. Opening night for the new 125th Street Apollo Theater was January 26, 1934, and featured the show "Jazz a la Carte" headlined by Benny Carter and his Orchestra, Ralph Cooper, and Aida Ward.

Over the years, the Apollo stage was lit up by Bessie Smith, Billie Holiday, Lena Horne, the Count Basie Orchestra, Duke Ellington, Dinah Washington, Charlie Parker, Dizzy Gillespie, Thelonious Monk, Aretha Franklin, and many other legendary performers.

Wednesdays were (and still are!) Amateur Night, when a merciless crowd either kills a performer's dreams or fulfills them. Sarah Vaughan, Pearl Bailey, James Brown, Gladys Knight and the Pips, Stevie Wonder, Michael Jackson, and Lauryn Hill all took their chances on Amateur Night and were launched from the Apollo.

3. Identity thieves often send fraudulent e-mail to lure victims into revealing confidential information. What is the term for this practice?
4. Scientists believe that life on Earth was originally cooked up in an organic ooze often referred to as "primeval" or "primordial" what?
5. In 2004, what company discovered that a Bic pen could be used to pick its popular U-shaped bike locks?
6. What type of data storage device invented in 1998 by IBM is often found attached to a key chain?

Ben's Double or Nothing Bonus

Knossos, the famed capital of the Minoan civilization, was allegedly home of the maze-dwelling minotaur, who was half man and half bull. This Bronze Age archaeological site is now a tourist highlight found on what Mediterranean island?

AND THE ANSWERS ARE . . .

$50 questions

1. Numerator
2. Flip-flops
3. Bronze Age
4. Leprechauns
5. (James T.) Kirk

Red Light Challenge 1

(Royal Dutch) Shell
ExxonMobil
BP (British Petroleum)
China National Petroleum
Chevron
Total
ConocoPhillips
6. Thin Mints

$100 questions

1. Emancipation Proclamation
2. Nave
3. Tripp
4. Doge
5. Amniotic fluid
6. Marmaduke

Red Light Challenge 2

Calgary (Flames)
Edmonton (Oilers)

Montreal (Canadiens)
Ottawa (Senators)
Quebec (Maple Leafs)
Vancouver (Canucks)
Winnipeg (Jets)

$200 questions

1. Keds
2. Ivan (III)
3. Phishing
4. Soup
5. Kryptonite (even Superman's bike was not safe)
6. Flash drive

Ben's Double or Nothing Bonus

Crete

74TH AND SECOND AVENUE
TO MADISON SQUARE GARDEN
(50 BLOCKS)

These questions are worth $50 each.

1. Let's start with a serious subject—beer technology. What Irish brew patented a special can to simulate the on-tap experience at a pub?
2. What Chinese-American martial arts icon died in 1973 at the young age of thirty-two?
3. Due to their anti-inflammatory properties, gold compounds are commonly injected into the body to treat what common joint disease?
4. In 2004, what pro sports league became the first to cancel an entire season due to a labor dispute?
5. From a Greek word meaning "to leave out," what astronomical event occurs when one celestial body moves into the shadow of another?

6. Derived from a Monty Python sketch, by what term is unsolicited junk e-mail commonly known?

7. If you get three wrong on *Cash Cab*, you're TKO'd. In boxing, what is TKO short for?

RED LIGHT CHALLENGE 1

This Red Light Challenge tests your mastery of the universe. In terms of total mass, name four of the five most common chemical elements in the universe. You have 30 seconds to earn $250.

8. What scale is used to measure the magnitude of earthquakes?

9. For over seventy years, the Rockettes have been getting their kicks at what New York City venue?

10. Still practiced by the Catholic Church, what ritual is used to drive evil spirits from an allegedly possessed human?

These questions are worth $100 each.

1. What famed nightclub owner shot and killed Lee Harvey Oswald, the assassin of John F. Kennedy?

2. In what George Orwell novel do barn dwellers declare, "Four legs good, two legs bad"?

3. After Hurricane Katrina devastated New Orleans' levees, what lake's water poured into the city?

4. What reptile lends its name to a popular type of candy made with caramel, pecans, and chocolate?

RED LIGHT CHALLENGE 2

This Red Light Challenge takes us back to the turn of the previous century. Name five of the six most populous U.S. cities in the year 1900.

5. What rival nation did Britain battle in the Seven Years' War, the Nine Years' War, and the Hundred Years' War?

6. Saudi Arabia banned what popular Japanese children's cards for allegedly promoting Zionism?

7. At the pet store, lionheads, bubble eyes, and fantails are all types of what?

8. In the world of cocktails, what sweet crimson syrup gives a Tequila Sunrise its trademark red glow?

MADISON SQUARE GARDEN

In 1906, the "Trial of the Century" involved a millionaire, a show-girl/artist's model and Stanford White, one of the world's most famous architects. And it all played out on the roof of the old Madison Square Garden—back when it was actually in Madison Square.

The basics: On June 25, while the chorus sang "I Could Love a Million Girls" at the premiere of the musical revue *Mam'zelle Champagne* at the Madison Square Roof Garden (a building White had designed), White was shot in the face and killed by Harry Kendall Thaw, the millionaire husband of Evelyn Nesbit. White, it seemed, *had* loved a million girls, including Nesbit five years earlier—back when she was sixteen and he was forty-seven.

Thaw was the jealous type, and after he married Nesbit, he pushed her for details of the affair. What he found out from her (and the rest of the world found out at Thaw's trial) was that White had a red velvet swing installed in his apartment, where Nesbit and other girls played "in varying degrees of undress." White also originated the now-famous invitation to come up to his rooms and see his etchings. (Every cliché starts somewhere.)

White was a partner in McKim, Mead & White, one of the top architecture firms in the world. He designed and decorated the Washington Square Arch and Fifth Avenue mansions for the Astors and the Vanderbilts. The firm's commissions included the Harvard Club, Metropolitan Club, Manhattan Municipal Building, Brooklyn Museum, New York Public Library, the old Penn Station, Morgan Library and Museum, and Hotel Pennsylvania.

Thaw was tried twice for the murder. The jury was deadlocked at the first trial, despite the fact that Thaw shot White point-blank in front of quite a few witnesses. At the second trial, he pleaded temporary insanity. Thaw's mother promised Nesbit that if she claimed White had raped her and that Thaw was trying to avenge her honor, she would receive a quiet divorce and $1 million. Nesbit testified, Thaw was acquitted, the divorce came next, but the ex–Mrs. Thaw never got a dime.

Thaw ended up at the Matteawan State Hospital for the Criminally Insane in Beacon, New York, which could not possibly have been a nice place in 1906. He tried to escape to Canada a couple of times, but was always brought back. In 1915 Thaw was released from custody after the doctors decided he wasn't crazy after all.

9. The self-proclaimed "King of Scotland," what Ugandan dictator named his kids McLaren, McKenzie, and Mackintosh?
10. Still educating after 369 years, what is America's oldest institution of higher learning?

These questions are worth $200 each.

1. According to the Bible, the dimensions of Noah's Ark were three hundred by fifty by thirty using what unit of measurement?
2. Immortalized on a postage stamp in 1995, what jukebox company's most famous model is nicknamed the "Bubbler"?
3. Used in some Native American religious ceremonies, what hallucinogen is extracted from the peyote cactus?

4. In Colonial America, air fresheners called "pomanders" were made by studding oranges with what nail-shaped spice?

5. Meaning "seven" in Yiddish, what traditional Jewish mourning period is observed by relatives of the deceased for a full week?

RED LIGHT CHALLENGE 3

If you get this Red Light Challenge right, you'll be pleased as punch. Name five of the six original flavors of Kool-Aid.

6. Fleeing scandal, Alberto Fujimori resigned as president of what South American nation in 2000 by sending a fax from Tokyo?

7. U.S. police departments buy more than 60 percent of their firearms from what Austrian gun maker?

8. On a stringed instrument like a guitar, the metal strips inserted on the fingerboard are called what?

9. If you're in a heated game of craps and the dice show "boxcars," what was your roll?

10. Though Chinese was her first language, what author of *The Good Earth* was America's first female Nobel Prize winner for literature?

HOW MANY TAXIS ARE THERE?

In 2010 there were 13,237 yellow cabs on the road in New York City. To give you an idea of how that fits into the flow of Manhattan traffic, seven out of ten cars on the road in Manhattan are taxis. About 250 million people ride in a New York City taxi each year. That's slightly more than the entire population of Indonesia—although it doesn't mean everyone in Indonesia came to New York to hail a cab.

Ben's Double or Nothing Bonus

California's beautiful Death Valley is the lowest point in North America. The highest point is a couple of thousand miles north in Alaska. Name this mountain.

$50 questions

1. Guinness
2. Bruce Lee
3. Arthritis
4. NHL (National Hockey League)
5. Eclipse
6. Spam
7. Technical knockout

Red Light Challenge 1

Hydrogen
Helium
Oxygen
Carbon
Neon

8. Richter scale
9. Radio City Music Hall
10. Exorcism

$100 questions

1. Jack Ruby
2. *Animal Farm*
3. Lake Pontchartrain
4. Turtle

Red Light Challenge 2

New York City
Chicago
Philadelphia

AND THE ANSWERS ARE . . .

Saint Louis
Boston
Baltimore

5. France
6. Pokemon
7. Goldfish
8. Grenadine
9. Idi Amin
10. Harvard University

$200 questions

1. Cubit
2. Wurlitzer
3. Mescaline
4. Cloves
5. Shiva

Red Light Challenge 3

Cherry
Grape
Lemon-Lime
Orange
Raspberry
Strawberry

6. Peru
7. Glock
8. Frets
9. Pair of sixes
10. Pearl S. Buck

Ben's Double or Nothing Bonus

Mt. McKinley

W 31st St
E 33rd St
E 32nd St
E 31st St
E 30th St
Morgan St
E River Dr
W 29th St
W 28th St
E 29th St
5th Ave
7th St
W 27th St
E 28th St
Avenue Of The Americas
Madison
Square
Park
E 26th St
E 25th St
W 24th St
W 25th St
elsen Waterside
W 23rd St
9th Ave
W 22nd St
E 23rd St
Park Ave S
Lexington Ave
Avenue A
E River Park
Avenue C
8th Ave
W 21st St
W 20th St
W 19th St
E 22nd
E 21st St
Gramercy Park
E 20th St
E 19th St
E 18th St
E 17th St
10th Ave
W 18th St
Broadway
W 17th St
W 16th St
7th Ave
5th Ave
Union
Square
E 16th St
E 15th St
Stuyvesant Square
1st Ave
E 14th St
Avenue B
E 14th St
E 15th St
Washington St
Hudson St
W 14th St
W 13th St
4th Ave
3rd Ave
E 13th St
E 12th St
Avenue C
Avenue C
W 12th St
9th Ave
5th Ave
University Pl
Irving Pl
Avenue D
E 10th St
E 11th St
E 10th St
E 9th St
E 8th St
Avenue A
Tompkins
Square
Park
Loisaida Ave
E 8th St
W 11th St
Bank St
7th Ave S
W 10th St
MacDougal St
St Marks Pl
E 7th St
E 6th St
Perry St
Morton St
Christopher St
6th Ave
Bleecker St
W 3rd St
Mercer St
Lafayette St
Bowery
E 5th St
E 4th St
E 3rd St
E 2nd St
2nd Ave
Clarkson St
Bleecker St
E 1st St
E Houston St
Ham
Fish
Varick St
Hudson St
Avenue Of The Americas
W Broadway
Greene St
Broadway
Prince St
Elizabeth St
Chrystie St
Allen St
Stanton St
Rivington St
Ludlow St
Essex St
Pitt St
Dela
Spring St
Mulberry St
Mott St
Bowery
Eldridge St
Broome St
Grand St
Laight St
Beach St
Broome St
Grand St
Lafayette St
E Broadway
Henry St
Seward
Park
Canal St
Baxter St
Hester St
Walker St
White St
Centre St
Bay
Madison St
Cherry St
E River Piers
FD
North River Piers
West St
Greenwich St
W Broadway
Leonard St
Duane St
Chambers St
Worth St
Thomas Paine
Park
Park Row
Catherine St
FDR
Manhattan Brg
Governor
son A Rockefeller
Park
N End Ave
Warren St
Church St
Murray St
City Hall Park
Frankfort St
Franklin D Roosevelt Dr
Turl
Vesey St
Ann St
North Cove
Liberty St
on Of Heroes
Nassau St
William St
Pearl St
Front St
South St
Brooklyn Brg
278
Albany St
Esplanade

AVENUE A AND 9TH STREET
TO 24TH AND NINTH AVENUE
(26 BLOCKS)

These questions are worth $50 each.

1. When smoked, what type of fish becomes lox?
2. Which of the Marx Brothers said volumes by never uttering a word on-screen?
3. In which Shakespeare play does the Prince of Denmark ask "to be or not to be"?
4. Endorsed by William Shatner, what Web site invites travelers to make bids on flights, hotel rooms, and rental cars?
5. Although its effectiveness is still unproven, what aromatic wood is traditionally used in closets to repel moths?
6. Ray Kroc opened the first franchise of what restaurant chain in California in 1955?

THE CHECKER CAB

Taxi models have come and gone, but none is more iconic than the Checker Cab—a big, boxy yellow car with a checkerboard-pattern racing stripe down the side and around the windows.

Taxi fleet owners usually also manufactured their own cars, so the large fleets were primarily owned by the big car makers like General Motors and Ford. But the biggest and most successful was the Checker Cab Manufacturing Company of Kalamazoo, Michigan. Checker was founded in 1922 by Morris Markin, a young Russian immigrant, and he ended up holding a near monopoly on cabs in New York (and in Chicago, Pittsburgh, and Minneapolis) for decades, simply because his cars were so good. During the 1920s there were more than seven thousand Checker cabs in New York.

Originally, New York taxis were required to hold five passengers behind the driver, and Checker cabs were big inside and out. The beginning of the end came in 1954, when New York authorized the use of smaller cabs. Drivers switched to cheaper cars that used less gas, and the Checker cabs slowly disappeared. The last Checker cab in New York was retired on July 26, 1999.

Checker Motors Corporation then began supplying parts to General Motors and other car companies. David Markin, Morris' son, took over the business and kept it going for a while. But trouble in the U.S. car industry hit the company hard, and in early 2010 the last assets were sold off and Checker closed. Those huge, boxy cabs are now considered collector's items and sell for a lot of money. After all, they cost less than a condo and are as big as a Manhattan studio apartment.

These questions are worth $100 each.

1. Cathy and Heathcliff are the star-crossed lovers at the center of what Emily Brontë novel?

2. In fashion, "YSL" refers to which French label?

3. What former Secretary of the Treasury was the principal author of The Federalist Papers?

4. Found in Venice, what kind of long, narrow boat is usually propelled by a standing oarsman?

RED LIGHT CHALLENGE 1

We're stopped at a red light, so it's time for a Red Light Challenge. Remember, this is worth $250.

J. Edgar Hoover ran the FBI under eight presidents. Name six of these eight commanders in chief. You have 30 seconds.

5. *Cash Cab* is all about measuring a person's I.Q., which is an abbreviation for what?

6. Finish this Thomas Edison quote: "Genius is 1 percent inspiration, 99 percent" what?

These questions are worth $200 each.

1. In the board game Clue, what educator is represented by the purple piece?
2. Abbreviated "HFCS," what processed sweetener does the average American consume over forty pounds of every year?

RED LIGHT CHALLENGE 2

This Red Light Challenge takes us on a brief trip Down Under. Name four of the five most populous cities in Australia.

3. Located near Washington, D.C., what military base is the home hangar of Air Force One?
4. Popular in Florida, what Spanish sport's players use custom-made wicker baskets to hurl a ball at one hundred fifty miles per hour?
5. Known as the "Father of the Atomic Bomb," who was the director of the legendary Manhattan Project?
6. Causing liquid to act as an elastic sheet, what property enables insects to walk on water?

Ben's Double or Nothing Bonus

In Japan, the star-shaped gonads of this spiky creature are considered a delicacy and an aphrodisiac. Called "uni" at a sushi bar, what is this prickly relative of the starfish?

$50 questions

1. Salmon
2. Harpo
3. *Hamlet*
4. Priceline (.com)
5. Cedar
6. McDonald's

$100 questions

1. *Wuthering Heights*
2. Yves Saint Laurent
3. Alexander Hamilton
4. Gondola

Red Light Challenge 1

(Calvin) Coolidge
(Herbert) Hoover
(Franklin) Roosevelt
(Harry) Truman
(Dwight) Eisenhower
(John) Kennedy
(Lyndon) Johnson
(Richard) Nixon

5. Intelligence Quotient
6. Perspiration

$200 questions

1. Professor Plum
2. High fructose corn syrup

AND THE ANSWERS ARE . . .

Red Light Challenge 2

Sydney
Melbourne
Brisbane
Perth
Adelaide

3. Andrews Air Force Base
4. Jai alai
5. (Robert) Oppenheimer
6. Surface tension

Ben's Double or Nothing Bonus

Sea urchin

E 33rd St
E 32nd St
E 31st St
E 30th St
W 29th St
W 28th St
E 28th St
E 29th St
W 27th St
5th Ave
E River Dr
Marginal St
W 25th St
W 24th St
Madison Square Park
Avenue Of The Americas
Park Ave S
Lexington Ave
E 26th St
E 25th St
E 24th St
W 23rd St
W 22nd St
W 21st St
W 20th St
E 23rd St
E 22nd St
E 21st St
E 23rd St
10th Ave
9th Ave
8th Ave
Broadway
W 19th St
W 18th St
W 17th St
W 16th St
W 15th St
Gramercy Park
E 20th St
E 19th St
E 18th St
E 17th St
Avenue C
E River Piers
Union Square
7th Ave
Irving Pl
Stuyvesant Square
E 15th St
E 14th St
W 14th St
E 14th St
E 15th St
Washington St
Hudson St
W 12th St
W 13th St
E 10th St
4th Ave
3rd Ave
1st Ave
Avenue B
Avenue C
E 12th St
E 11th St
W 11th St
7th Ave S
6th Ave
5th Ave
University Pl
E 10th St
E 9th St
E 8th St
Avenue A
Tompkins Square Park
E 8th St
Bank St
Perry St
W 10th St
St Marks Pl
E 7th St
E 6th St
Christopher St
MacDougal St
Mercer St
Lafayette St
E 5th St
Loisaida Ave
W 3rd St
E 4th St
Bowery
2nd Ave
E 3rd St
Morton St
7th Ave S
Bleecker St
Bleecker St
E 2nd St
Clarkson St
E Houston St
E 1st St
Varick St
6th Ave
W Broadway
Greene St
Broadway
Prince St
Elizabeth St
Chrystie St
Avenue Of The Immigrants
Stanton St
Rivington St
Pitt St
Hudson St
Spring St
Ludlow St
Broome St
Lafayette St
Mulberry St
Mott St
Bowery
Allen St
Broome St
Grand St
Essex St
Grand St
Canal St
Avenue Of The Americas
Eldridge St
E Broadway
Henry St
Laight St
Walker St
Baxter St
Hester St
Seward Park
Beach St
N River Piers
West St
Greenwich St
W Broadway
White St
Centre St
Madison St
Leonard St
Worth St
Catherine St
Market St
Cherry St
E River Piers
Duane St
Thomas Paine Park
Chambers St
Park Row
Warren St
Governor Nelson A Rockefeller Park
N End Ave
Murray St
Church St
City Hall Park
Frankfort St
Franklin D Roosevelt Dr
Manhattan Brg
Vesey St
Ann St
Pearl St
Brooklyn Brg
North Cove
Liberty St
Nassau St
William St
Albany St
Trinity
Pearl St
Front St
South St
278

CHRISTOPHER AND BLEECKER STREETS
TO AVENUE C AND 12TH
(19 BLOCKS)

These questions are worth $50 each.

1. Shunned by charcoal traditionalists, "liquefied petroleum" is another term for what grill-friendly gas?
2. Sometimes eliciting an LOL, what two-word phrase is abbreviated "JK" in the world of texting?
3. What president's diaries, posthumously published in 2007, include the revelation that "getting shot hurts"?
4. Honda's answer to the Lexus, what luxury car's logo features calipers in the shape of the letter A?

These questions are worth $100 each.

1. Debuting in Batman comic book #16, what is the name of Bruce Wayne's trusty butler/assistant?

RED LIGHT CHALLENGE

This is a real dickens of a Red Light Challenge. Name four of the five Charles Dickens novels that made the BBC's list of the one hundred best-loved novels of all time. Remember, you have 30 seconds to earn $250.

2. What cereal company has its headquarters in Battle Creek, Michigan?
3. First held in 1877, what kennel club's annual dog show takes place right here in New York, at Madison Square Garden?
4. What accounting firm has been tabulating and certifying Academy Awards votes for more than seventy years?

BEN'S FAVORITE SPOTS IN THE VILLAGE

New York is a big city made up of small neighborhoods, and Greenwich Village is my favorite. I love just walking around the Village and people watching. But I also have some favorite places. Here are a couple of them.

Famous Ben's Pizza of SoHo

Okay, so technically it's not in the Village, but this place on Spring Street and Thompson just has the best pizza. I love it. And not because we have the same name.

The Minettas

Minetta Lane runs from Sixth Avenue to MacDougal Street, and Minetta Street starts at Minetta Lane and somehow winds up at Sixth and Bleecker. There also used to be a Minetta Place and a Minetta Court, but they've been gone since at least the 1930s. The Minettas originally followed Minetta Brook, which rises at about Sixth Avenue and 21st and wanders southwest to drain into the Hudson. The brook was submerged in the 1820s, but still makes its presence known in local basements after a heavy rain.

MUD Coffee Truck

It's usually parked at Sheridan Square, at Barrow Street and West 4th. This is the best cup of coffee in New York. The owners make their own secret blend, and the coffee is always strong but not bitter. You can also get bagels, croissants, or a MUD T-shirt—very New York.

The Comedy Cellar/Olive Tree Café

The Comedy Cellar on MacDougal Street between West 3rd and Minetta Lane is my regular home club, so if you stop by you might see me there. The owners are good friends of mine, and the food upstairs at the Olive Tree is great and cheap and they're open really late.

These questions are worth $200 each.

1. Fifty years before Watergate, the Harding administration suffered its own scandal involving what Wyoming oil reserve?
2. What New Age concept that means "circle" in Sanskrit refers to centers of psychic energy in the body?
3. Liar's Poker, a popular bluffing bar game, is played with what substitute for cards?
4. Comprising three fatty acids, what category of fats is commonly measured as part of a typical cholesterol test?

Ben's Double or Nothing Bonus

In a constant state of eruption since 1983, this chain smoker is said to be the world's most active volcano. Emitting up to two thousand tons of volcanic smoke and ash per day, what is the name of this U.S. hot spot?

$50 questions

1. Propane
2. Just kidding
3. (Ronald) Reagan
4. Acura

$100 questions

1. Alfred (Pennyworth)

Red Light Challenge

A Christmas Carol
Bleak House
David Copperfield
Great Expectations
A Tale of Two Cities

2. Kellogg's
3. Westminster (Kennel Club)
4. PricewaterhouseCoopers (Price Waterhouse, which is what it used to be called before Coopers moved in, is also acceptable.)

$200 questions

1. Teapot Dome
2. Chakras
3. Dollar bills
4. Triglycerides

Ben's Double or Nothing Bonus

Kilauea (in Hawaii)

AND THE ANSWERS ARE . . .

E 33rd St
E 32nd St
E 31st St
E 30th St
W 29th St
W 28th St
E 29th St
W 27th St
E 28th St
5th Ave
W 24th St
W 25th St
Madison Square Park
Park Ave S
Lexington Ave
E 26th St
E 25th St
E 24th St
W 23rd St
W 22nd St
W 21st St
W 20th St
Avenue Of The Americas
Broadway
E 23rd St
E 22nd St
E 21st St
Gramercy Park
E 20th St
10th Ave
9th Ave
8th Ave
W 19th St
W 18th St
W 17th St
W 16th St
W 15th St
E 19th St
E 18th St
E 17th St
Union Square
Irving Pl
Stuyvesant Square
E 15th St
E 14th St
W 14th St
7th Ave
Hudson St
Washington St
W 12th St
W 13th St
E 13th St
University Pl
4th Ave
3rd Ave
1st Ave
E 14th St
E 15th St
E 12th St
E 11th St
W 11th St
Bank St
Perry St
W 10th St
7th Ave S
5th Ave
E 10th St
E 9th St
E 8th St
Avenue A
Avenue B
Avenue C
Tompkins Square Park
E 8th St
St Marks Pl
E 7th St
E 6th St
Christopher St
MacDougal St
W 3rd St
Mercer St
Lafayette St
E 5th St
E 4th St
E 3rd St
E 2nd St
Bowery
2nd Ave
Loisaida Ave
Morton St
Bleecker St
Clarkson St
E Houston St
E 1st St
Stanton St
Rivington St
Varick St
6th Ave
W Broadway
Greene St
Prince St
Spring St
Elizabeth St
Chrystie St
Avenue Of The Immigrants
Ludlow St
Pitt St
Broome St
Grand St
Mott St
Mulberry St
Allen St
Essex St
Canal St
Laight St
Walker St
Hester St
Eldridge St
Baxter St
E Broadway
Henry St
Seward Park
Beach St
White St
Centre St
West St
N River Piers
Greenwich St
Leonard St
Duane St
Worth St
Thomas Paine Park
Madison St
Cherry St
E River Piers
Market St
Catherine St
Park Row
Chambers St
Warren St
N End Ave
City Hall Park
Franklin D Roosevelt Dr
Manhattan Brg
Murray St
Church St
Frankfort St
Vesey St
Ann St
Brooklyn Brg
North Cove
Liberty St
Pearl St
Nassau St
William St
Albany St
Front St
South St
278

SECOND AVENUE AND 116TH STREET TO 187TH STREET AND BROADWAY (66 BLOCKS)

These questions are worth $50 each.

1. To cover up the fact that it was using radar (then a top secret technology) in World War II, the British Royal Air Force attributed the sharp night vision of its pilots to a diet rich in what vegetable?
2. What musician named his kids Dweezil, Moon Unit, Ahmet, and Diva?
3. Commonly used to clean car windows, what rubber-bladed tool is also used in screen printing?
4. In what city is Old North Church, where lanterns were hung to guide Paul Revere?
5. What modern country was once home to the ancient Aztecs?

6. If you're choosing between Virgin and Extra Virgin, what cooking ingredient are you shopping for?
7. What is the name of the talking computer in Stanley Kubrick's *2001: A Space Odyssey*?
8. Women go crazy for Manolo Blahnik, not because of his looks but because he designs what?

RED LIGHT CHALLENGE 1

Traffic has stopped, and it's time for a Red Light Challenge. This is worth $250.

Mandated by the FDA, the Nutrition Facts Label on all packaged foods lists quantities of six categories in big, bold-faced type. Name five of these six categories. You have 30 seconds.

These questions are worth $100 each.

1. Popularized by educator Thomas Gallaudet, what language is abbreviated "ASL"?
2. What endangered species of crane, named for its distinctive call, can be heard up to two miles away?
3. A clue to its historical ties to plumbing, what metallic element is abbreviated PB on the Periodic Table?

4. Taking over in 2008, what Cuban president is said to have less charisma and less facial hair than his big brother?
5. Named for its country of origin, what infamous 1980s import was voted "Worst Car of the Millennium" by NPR's *Car Talk*?
6. On his seventieth birthday, what "Father of Fitness" towed seventy boats carrying seventy people for a mile and a half?

RED LIGHT CHALLENGE 2

This Red Light Challenge is very important to cab-drivers. According to Carspace.com, what are four of the five essential fluids in your car that should be checked regularly?
   This is worth $250.

7. Made mainly of minerals, what tough outer layer of dental tissue does not regenerate when damaged?
8. As she often reminds viewers, what cable TV personality became a prosecutor after the murder of her fiancé?

ALL HAIL

Sometimes it's impossible to get a cab in New York. But it is getting easier. Starting in 2006, cabs were all fitted with GPS devices, which means if you have a satellite, you know where they are. If you don't have a satellite, an iPhone or Android phone will do. Both now offer an application called CabSense, developed by some deep thinkers at MIT and Columbia University, that, according to Cab-Sense, uses street corner ratings "derived from machine learning algorithms applied to tens of millions of historical location points from the pickups and drop-offs of all New York City taxicabs. Every street corner in the city is rated from five stars (best corners to hail an open cab) to half a star (low chance to hail an open cab). Corners with historically very few taxi pickups don't get any stars at all. These ratings change based on the time of day and the day of the week." (Please do not ask for a translation of that!)

The free app includes a map of your current location, a radar view that points you to the best street corner to hail a cab, a time slider so you can plan where to hail a cab later, and a cab hailer that sends out a loud whistle when you shake your phone.

So that iconic New York pose—people standing in the street with one arm raised like the Statue of Liberty to hail a cab—may one day morph into people standing on street corners shaking their phones. Let's hope not.

These questions are worth $200 each.

1. Coined by French physiologist Charles Richet, what you gonna call the slimy substance excreted by ghosts?

2. With cleverness to spare, what bowling alley company chose "PIN" as its stock market symbol?

3. Meaning "mouse's mouth" in Spanish, what Florida city's aging population has earned it the nickname "God's waiting room"?

RED LIGHT CHALLENGE 3

Another red light, another Red Light Challenge.
In the NFL, four teams feature felines in their team names. Name all four of these big cats of the gridiron.

4. What term, abbreviated "UGC," refers to the homegrown material found on Web sites like YouTube and Wikipedia?

5. Promising a larger payout than a trifecta, what specific wager requires you to pick the top four finishers in a horse race?

6. A full moon occurs when the moon is farthest from the sun. What phase occurs when it is closest?

7. Held in East Dublin, Georgia, what irreverent annual games feature bobbing for pig's trotters, hubcap hurling, and toilet seat throwing?

8. What cabinet-level position created in 2003 is last in the line of presidential succession?

Ben's Double or Nothing Bonus

The Statue of Liberty is an American icon, but it was created by two Frenchmen. The statue's skin sculptor was Frédéric-Auguste Bartholdi, and her skeleton was designed by what French engineer who later became famous for a landmark of his own?

AND THE ANSWERS ARE . . .

$50 questions

1. Carrots
2. Frank Zappa
3. Squeegee
4. Boston
5. Mexico
6. Olive oil
7. HAL (Have you forgotten me already, Dave?)
8. Shoes

Red Light Challenge 1

Calories
(Total) Fat
Cholesterol
Sodium
(Total) Carbohydrates
Protein

$100 questions

1. American Sign Language
2. Whooping crane
3. Lead
4. Raul Castro (Just "Castro" doesn't count here!)
5. Yugo
6. Jack LaLanne

Red Light Challenge 2

Engine oil
Transmission fluid
Brake fluid
Window washer fluid
Engine coolant (antifreeze)

7. Enamel
8. Nancy Grace

$200 questions

1. Ectoplasm
2. AMF (Bowling)
3. Boca Raton

Red Light Challenge 3

(Cincinnati) Bengals
(Detroit) Lions
(Jacksonville) Jaguars
(North Carolina) Panthers

4. User-generated content
5. Superfecta
6. New moon
7. The Redneck Games (These are the Summer Redneck Games, of course.)
8. Secretary of Homeland Security

Ben's Double or Nothing Bonus

(Gustave) Eiffel

BOWERY AND BAYARD
TO 18TH STREET AND FIRST AVENUE
(28 BLOCKS)

These questions are worth $50 each.

1. Meaning "head wiggle" in Middle English, a pollywog is another word for what immature animal?
2. "Brothers in Arms" by Dire Straits was the first album to sell a million copies in what format?

RED LIGHT CHALLENGE 1

Here's your 30-second, $250 Red Light Challenge.
The African Union specifically identifies six official languages in its charter. Name five of these six languages.

3. What building rises more than fourteen hundred feet above the Chicago skyline?
4. Thin Mints, Samoas, and Tagalongs are all delicious cookies sold by what organization?
5. What redheaded comic book character has friends named Jughead, Veronica, and Betty?

These questions are worth $100 each.

1. Which chapter of the U.S. Bankruptcy Code governs the process of reorganization?
2. On the TV show *Mythbusters,* radar technology was used to determine whether Jimmy Hoffa is buried in the end zone of what stadium?
3. Meaning "good" in Tahitian, what supposedly Polynesian cocktail is actually a California concoction from Trader Vic's?
4. Located at the tip of Spain, what resilient rock is depicted in the logo for Prudential Insurance?
5. Named for "the homeliest gal" in *Li'l Abner,* on what special day do girls traditionally ask boys to a dance?

RED LIGHT CHALLENGE 2

At the Summer Olympics, eight track-and-field events are considered purely "field" competitions. Name seven of these eight events.

BEN'S FAVORITE NEW YORK SUBWAY STATIONS

I can't imagine why you'd take a subway when there are plenty of cabs aboveground waiting to drive you wherever you want to go. But the New York City subway system has 468 stations, and some of them are actually worth looking at. Here are four of my favorites.

14th Street and Eighth Avenue

Sculptor Tom Otterness' Life Underground is made up of more than fifty bronze figures scattered all over the station and doing subversive things like sneaking in under the barrier and sawing down the stairway supports. There's even that quintessential New York icon—an alligator emerging from the sewer.

Museum of Natural History, 81st Street and Central Park West

The lowest levels have casts of the museum's famous dinosaur fossils, and the casts and mosaics work their way up in time and evolution as you climb the stairs. The images of mammals, insects, and reptiles are all over the place, so don't forget to look at the floors.

Lincoln Center, 66th Street and Broadway

The walls are decorated with shiny golden mosaics by Nancy Spero, and feature opera singers, ballet dancers, acrobats, and just some weird figures doing who knows what—but in a very artistic way.

42nd Street and Bryant Park

The tunnel that connects the platform for the 7 train to the F train platform is the thing here. It's lined with an amazing mosaic called Under Bryant Park by Samm Kunce that shows all the roots and bedrock that were dug away to make room for the subway.

These questions are worth $200 each.

1. What household appliance did Isaac Singer improve in the 1800s by adding a presser foot?
2. An "Eskimo roll" is a maneuver used to turn over what kind of capsized watercraft?
3. What seven-minute Beatles song was written for John Lennon's first son?
4. What communist country, bordered by Thailand and Vietnam, has Vientiane as its capital?
5. What young Illinois senator delivered the keynote speech at the 2004 Democratic National Convention?

Ben's Double or Nothing Bonus

Hot on the heels of Halloween, this macabre Mexican holiday is observed with sugar skulls, chocolate coffins, and elaborate graveside decorations. What is the name of this annual spook-filled celebration?

$50 questions

1. Tadpole
2. Compact disc

Red Light Challenge 1

Arabic
English
French
Spanish
Portuguese
Swahili (or Kiswahili)

3. Sears Tower
4. Girl Scouts
5. Archie

$100 questions

1. Chapter 11
2. Giants Stadium
3. Mai Tai
4. (Rock of) Gibraltar
5. Sadie Hawkins Day

Red Light Challenge 2

Long jump
Triple jump
High jump
Pole vault
Shot put

AND THE ANSWERS ARE . . .

Discus
Javelin
Hammer throw

$200 questions

1. Sewing machine
2. Kayak
3. "Hey Jude"
4. Laos
5. Barack Obama

Ben's Double or Nothing Bonus

Day of the Dead

38TH AND MADISON TO AMSTERDAM
AND CATHEDRAL PARKWAY
(77 BLOCKS)

These questions are worth $50 each.

1. Let's start with a little *Cash Cab* geometry. What's the term for a triangle with three sides of the same length?
2. The Tropic of Cancer lies north of the equator. Which tropic lies south?
3. With twice as many neck vertebrae as humans, what nocturnal bird can rotate its head up to 270 degrees?
4. What Japanese word describes a great sea wave caused by an earthquake?
5. In April 2005, Joseph Ratzinger received the ultimate promotion to what lofty position?
6. Caused by burst blood vessels, what visible, subdermal mark is playfully referred to as a "love-bite"?

7. Since 2003, what Chinese cooking vessel has been used in an oddball annual sledding competition in Germany?
8. What type of paper made from the cannabis plant did Thomas Jefferson use to draft the Declaration of Independence?

RED LIGHT CHALLENGE 1

We're stopped at a red light, so it's time for a Red Light Challenge. Remember, this is worth $250.

Seven countries in the world today have official names that start with the letter U. You have 30 seconds to name five of them.

THE WAGES OF DRIVING

New York City ranks among the top thirty cities in the nation for average annual salary earned by taxi drivers and chauffeurs. But when you look at the numbers, a taxi is not really a Cash Cab for the driver. The mean hourly wage (that's mean as in average, but it is pretty mean) for a New York City cab driver is $13.17, with the top-earning 10 percent making $19.42 or more an hour and the bottom 10 percent earning $8.18 per hour or less. Taxi drivers in New York work an average of 52.2 hours a week and make $29,048 a year.

9. What famous Abbott and Costello routine features a pitcher named Tomorrow and a catcher named Today?
10. What type of drink was allegedly invented by a monk named Dom Perignon?

These questions are worth $100 each.

1. Featuring a rather odd breakfast, what 1960 Dr. Seuss book uses only fifty different words?
2. What British city welcomes tourists at John Lennon Airport with the slogan, "Above us only sky"?
3. By what title is Tibetan spiritual leader Tenzin Gyatso better known?
4. What legendary bank-robbing couple was gunned down on May 23, 1934?
5. A frozen favorite of Hemingway, what rum-and-lime cocktail is named for a mining village in Cuba?
6. What literary device is "Sing a song of sixpence," where successive words begin with the same letter?
7. The answer to this next question is neither Istanbul nor Constantinople. Since 1923, what city has served as the capital of Turkey?
8. In what famous Franz Kafka work did Gregor Samsa literally bug out?
9. What type of hot red pepper is named for the equally hot capital of French Guiana?

BEN'S FAVORITE HIDDEN MANHATTAN CEMETERIES

I'm not a ghoulish guy, but I do love the tiny, tucked-away cemeteries in Manhattan because they're quiet and almost invisible and they give us a little slice of a history that's usually been forgotten. All of these cemeteries are really hidden away, so you'll need to use some dead reckoning to find them.

New York Marble Cemetery

On Second Avenue between 2nd and 3rd Streets is the arched gate for this 1831 cemetery that's all underground burial vaults. There are no headstones: the dead are identified by inscriptions on slabs set into the walls.

New York City Marble Cemetery

This is a different Marble Cemetery, improbably located on 2nd Street between First and Second Avenues. President James Monroe was buried here for twenty-seven years, then dug up and reburied in the President's Circle at the Hollywood Cemetery in Richmond, Virginia. One person who is still here is Preserved Fish. Before you start giggling, Preserved is a very respectable Quaker name, as in "preserved in grace." And in New York State, Fish is a fairly common surname.

Cemetery of Shearith Israel

This very first Jewish congregation in New York was formed by refugees from Brazil in 1654. Shearith Israel has three cemeteries scattered around Manhattan, marking the movement of the congregation uptown. The oldest dates to 1683 and is at St. James Place just off Chatham Square in Chinatown. Revolutionary War veterans are among its permanent residents. The second is on West 11th

Street just east of Sixth Avenue, and started accepting guests from 1805. The third is on 21st Street between Sixth and Seventh Avenues, and opened in 1829. It had to shut its gates in 1852 when a city law was passed that said no one could be buried in Manhattan anymore.

10. Resigning amid scandal in 1973, Vice President Spiro Agnew was succeeded by what thirteen-term congressman from Michigan?

These questions are worth $200 each.

1. Founded by a rabbi in Cincinnati, what company is famous for its matzo and its kosher Concord Grape wine?
2. In forensic odontology, what part of the anatomy is studied to help identify a victim?
3. In a twisted tragedy by Sophocles, Oedipus turns out to be both the daddy *and* big brother of what unlucky heroine?
4. In physics, what is the term for an atom or a group of atoms with an electrical charge?
5. Telemark is not an annoying dinnertime phone call, but a specific type of turn in what sport?
6. Eclipsing McDonald's in 2001, what fast-food chain has the most locations in the United States?

RED LIGHT CHALLENGE 2

In the Cash Cab, it's Christmas all year round. To celebrate, name the six birds mentioned in the song "The 12 Days of Christmas."

7. Lending its name to a cropped jacket for women and an orchestral work by Ravel, what is the national dance of Spain?

8. According to the Bible, the Three Wise Men brought Jesus gold, myrrh, and what third aromatic gift?

9. Meaning "great madness" in Greek, what personality disorder is characterized by delusions of grandeur?

10. Starbucks coffee was named after a character in what famous Herman Melville novel?

Ben's Double or Nothing Bonus

Now as busy as Grand Central Terminal, the South Pole was no-man's-land until Roald Amundsen reached it in 1911. This lonely locale lies on a plateau in Antarctica that Amundsen named for Haakon VII, the reigning king of what nation?

$50 questions

1. Equilateral
2. Tropic of Capricorn
3. Owl
4. Tsunami
5. Pope
6. Hickey
7. Wok
8. Hemp

Red Light Challenge 1

Uganda
Ukraine
United Arab Emirates
United Kingdom
United States
Uruguay
Uzbekistan

9. "Who's on First?"
10. Champagne

$100 questions

1. *Green Eggs and Ham*
2. Liverpool
3. Dalai Lama
4. Bonnie and Clyde
5. Daiquiri
6. Alliteration

AND THE ANSWERS ARE . . .

7. Ankara
8. *Metamorphosis*
9. Cayenne
10. Gerald Ford

$200 questions

1. Manischewitz
2. Teeth
3. Antigone
4. Ion
5. Skiing
6. Subway

Red Light Challenge 2

Swans
Geese
Calling birds
French hens
Turtledoves
Partridge

7. Bolero
8. Frankincense
9. Megalomania
10. *Moby-Dick*

Ben's Double or Nothing Bonus

Norway

28TH STREET AND NINTH
TO LINCOLN CENTER
(35 BLOCKS)

These questions are worth $50 each.

1. Like cobras, crocodiles, and calculating killers, most sharks are ectotherms. "Ectothermic" is the scientific term for what characteristic?
2. A Las Vegas museum with exhibits that include a mink cape and a rhinestone-studded car pays tribute to what famed pianist?
3. Introduced by Procter & Gamble in 1968, what "newfangled chips" alleged that "Once you pop, you can't stop"?
4. What colorful term describes a city district in which brothels and other erotic businesses are concentrated?

LINCOLN CENTER

West Side Story begins with a sweeping shot of a run-down New York neighborhood, supposedly the turf of the Jets and Sharks. If you go looking for that neighborhood today, you won't find it. But it wasn't filmed on a back lot. It was filmed on the Upper West Side, where Lincoln Center is now.

In 1960 the whole area was condemned and the buildings were scheduled to be demolished. But demolition was put on hold for the movie.

In 1961 *West Side Story* won ten Oscars. And today, the area around Lincoln Center is crowded with luxury apartments that only movie stars can afford.

These questions are worth $100 each.

1. The Satin Dolls, located on New Jersey's Route 17, provided the setting for what fictional *Sopranos* strip club?
2. Despite its Alpine name, what leafy variety of beet has its roots in Sicily?
3. Roughing up rodents for more than fifty years, what household brand claims to be "America's #1 Brand of Mouse Killer"?
4. The name of what publishing company was inspired by an inside joke about the haphazard selection of its titles?

These questions are worth $200 each.

1. What delicacy of raw fish marinated in citrus

RED LIGHT CHALLENGE

Remember, this Red Light Challenge is worth $250.
Since 1933, a beverage called V8 has graced supermarket shelves. Name six of the eight veggies that make up V8 vegetable juice. You've got 30 seconds to get through six servings of vegetables.

juice, onions, and chilies is the national dish of Peru?

2. Because of child labor concerns, Qatar has adopted the use of robotic jockeys in what Middle Eastern sport?

3. Canada's answer to Wall Street, Bay Street is located in the financial district of what city?

4. Patented by Charles Goodyear in 1844, what chemical process do we have to thank for rubber tires and hockey pucks?

Ben's Double or Nothing Bonus

Located in Washington State, this supersized dam that harnesses the free-flowing power of the Columbia River used up enough concrete to circle the Equator—twice. What is the name of this massive dam?

$50 questions

1. Cold-bloodedness
2. Liberace
3. Pringles
4. Red light district

$100 questions

1. Bada Bing
2. Swiss chard
3. d-CON
4. Random House

Red Light Challenge

Beets
Celery
Carrots
Lettuce
Parsley
Spinach
Tomatoes
Watercress

$200 questions

1. Ceviche
2. Camel racing
3. Toronto
4. Vulcanization

Ben's Double or Nothing Bonus

Grand Coulee Dam

AND THE ANSWERS ARE . . .

NORFOLK AND RIVINGTON STREETS
TO 30TH STREET AND THIRD AVENUE
(35 BLOCKS)

These questions are worth $50 each.

1. With a name that's Greek for "river horse," what large African mammal typically surfaces to breathe once every three to five minutes?

2. Udon, ramen, and soba are all Japanese varieties of what food?

3. After twenty-seven years of incarceration, who was freed from a South African prison on February 11, 1990?

4. With its famous fifty-foot-high letters, what hillside L.A. landmark was originally a sign for a real estate company?

5. In 1903, what expert in radiation became the first woman to win the Nobel Prize in Physics?

6. Protecting breakables since 1957, "air cellular cushioning material" is a less common name for what clear plastic staple of shipping?

RED LIGHT CHALLENGE 1

This Red Light Challenge tests how good your poker face is. Name the five best hands you can have in a game of poker with no wild cards. You have 30 seconds to earn $250.

These questions are worth $100 each.

1. In the year 64, what mentally unstable emperor sat idle as Rome burned?
2. Named after gold medalist Dick Fosbury, what high jump technique put an end to the headfirst dive?
3. With about 40 million units sold, the Genesis and the Dreamcast were bestselling video game consoles from what company?
4. Used to thwart bank robbers and bad nannies, what type of video surveillance system is abbreviated "CCTV"?
5. According to Arctic legend, what celestial phenomenon represents spirits playing soccer with a frozen walrus skull?

6. Also a tiny blood vessel in the body, what type of action is used by paper towels to suck up water?

ELECTRIC CABS

Hybrid taxis are just starting to make inroads on the streets of New York. But the first taxis that weren't powered by horses were actually run on electric batteries. In fact, the first cab company in New York City was the Electric Carriage and Wagon Company, which started in July 1897 with twelve hansom cabs that they stuck batteries on. The batteries weighed more than 800 pounds, but despite that little impediment, by 1899 there were nearly one hundred electric cabs on the streets of New York.

By the early 1900s, the Electric Vehicle Company (just the renamed Electric Carriage and Wagon Company) was running one thousand electric taxicabs on the streets of New York City. But in January of 1907, a fire destroyed three hundred of these vehicles. There was also a stock market crash in October of that year, known as the Panic of 1907 (to distinguish it from other times people have panicked about the stock market). Meanwhile, gasoline-powered cabs were proving to be quite a bit less heavy. By 1910, all the electric cabs were gone, and in 1912 the Electric Vehicle Company went out of business.

These questions are worth $200 each.

1. Since 1930, what series of detective novels has been penned by numerous writers under the pseudonym Carolyn Keene?

2. In physics, a stone resting on a cliff's edge is said to possess what type of energy?
3. In 1988, Benazir Bhutto became the first female prime minister of what nation?
4. What famous gem did Harry Winston donate to the Smithsonian in 1958?

RED LIGHT CHALLENGE 2

Time to judge your knowledge of our government's judicial branch. Name six of the nine current justices of the U.S. Supreme Court.

5. FDR visited what Georgia city in hopes of improving the paralysis caused by polio?
6. Bisexual flowers are known as "perfect flowers" because they contain both pistils and what?

Ben's Double or Nothing Bonus

Fireworks were first created in China more than eleven thousand years ago. We owe their existence to the Chinese invention of what fast-burning substance used as a propellant in firearms?

$50 questions

1. Hippopotamus
2. Noodles
3. Nelson Mandela
4. Hollywood sign
5. Marie Curie
6. Bubble wrap

Red Light Challenge 1

Flush
Four of a kind
Full house
Royal (straight) flush
Straight flush

$100 questions

1. Nero
2. Fosbury flop
3. Sega
4. Closed-circuit television
5. Aurora borealis
6. Capillary

$200 questions

1. Nancy Drew
2. Potential energy (kind of like the Cash Cab stuck in traffic)

AND THE ANSWERS ARE...

3. Pakistan
4. Hope Diamond

Red Light Challenge 2

(Samuel) Alito
(Stephen) Breyer
(Ruth Bader) Ginsburg
(Elena) Kagan
(Anthony) Kennedy
(John) Roberts
(Antonin) Scalia
(Sonia) Sotomayor
(Clarence) Thomas

5. Warm Springs
6. Stamens

Ben's Double or Nothing Bonus

Gunpowder

TIMES SQUARE
TO 96TH AND BROADWAY
(57 BLOCKS)

These questions are worth $50 each.

1. Kangaroos are part of what group of mammals that typically carry their offspring in a pouch?
2. Cartoonist Thomas Nast is credited with creating the look of what jolly seasonal icon?
3. With thirty-four letters, what is the atrociously long song title from *Mary Poppins*?
4. What designer founded the fashion company known as DKNY?
5. Abbreviated "BBB," what watchdog organization was originally called the National Vigilance Committee?
6. Though not legal tender itself, what white, coin-shaped seashell is featured on banknotes in the Bahamas?

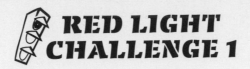

RED LIGHT CHALLENGE 1

Traffic means a Red Light Challenge. Remember, this is worth $250.

While Missouri is home to the Cardinals baseball team, seven of its neighbors claim the cardinal as their state bird. Name five of these seven cardinal states. You have 30 seconds.

7. What screen queen became true royalty when she married Monaco's Prince Rainier in 1956?

8. Founded in Germany in 1931, what sports car company's models include the Carrera and the Boxster?

HIGHER EDUCATION

How well would New York City taxi drivers do on *Cash Cab*? Not bad at all, if you go by their education level. Thirty-eight percent of drivers have been to college and 39 percent have a high school diploma.

These questions are worth $100 each.

1. On what date did both Thomas Jefferson and John Adams die in 1826?

2. Similar to parsley, what potent and poisonous herb was Socrates sentenced to drink in 399 B.C.E.?

3. Four North Carolina students made civil rights history in 1960 by staging a sit-in at the lunch counter of what store?

4. Though Duke Edward VIII preferred a wider knot on his tie, what triangular-style knot is named for him?

RED LIGHT CHALLENGE 2

In its first year, the Big Band and Jazz Hall of Fame honored five famous performers or bandleaders. Name four of these musician icons.

5. How were Presidents Franklin Delano Roosevelt and Teddy Roosevelt related?

6. Salt, pepper, flowers, and fresh mint are the ingredients in a fourth-century Egyptian recipe for what toiletry?

7. Now called Thailand, this Southeast Asian country joined Japan to declare war on the Allies in 1942. Back then, by what name was it known?

8. What popular variety of green apple did Australian Maria Ana Smith accidentally create in the 1860s?

THE BALL IN TIMES SQUARE

Millions of people all over the world tune in to watch a big crystal ball slide down a pole in Times Square at the start of each New Year. It's probably the most-watched pole dance in the world.

Ever wonder how all that got started? It was 1904 and the first subway line opened, running up Broadway. The *New York Times* also opened its new headquarters, and the owner, Alfred Ochs, decided to throw a New Year's Eve party. The Times Tower was set on a triangle of land called Longacre Square where Seventh Avenue, Broadway, and 42nd Street converge, and Ochs had already convinced the city to rename it Times Square. Now he threw an all-day block party to which everyone in New York was invited. More than 200,000 people showed up, and at midnight they were treated to a fireworks display set off from the base of the Times Tower. A tradition was born.

Two years later, the city banned the fireworks display as being too dangerous. So Ochs arranged to have a large, seven-hundred-pound iron and wood ball studded with lightbulbs lowered from the flagpole at the top of the Times Tower precisely at midnight to start 1908. Another tradition was born.

These questions are worth $200 each.

1. What famous house designed by Frank Lloyd Wright is perched over a river in Fayette County, Pennsylvania?
2. With only five people per square mile, what Asian neighbor of Russia is the least densely populated country in the world?

3. George Washington and Ben Franklin were both members of what fraternal organization?
4. It may be hip to be square, but how many sides does a heptagon have?
5. Named for a specific variety of raptor, the sport of using birds of prey for hunting is known as what?

RED LIGHT CHALLENGE 3

Another red light, another Red Light Challenge.
One of the world's longest rivers, the Mekong was once a major artery of the Angkor Empire. Name four of the six countries it flows through.

6. Also called the "Chicago typewriter," what submachine gun is a common fixture in gangster movies?
7. Agoraphobia is not a fear of sweaters, but of what?
8. According to Greek mythology, who led the Argonauts in their search for the golden fleece?

Ben's Double or Nothing Bonus

This well-equipped crustacean attracts the ladies by waving around its single, oversized claw. Named for its resemblance to a musician at work, what is this well-known species of crab?

$50 questions

1. Marsupials
2. Santa Claus
3. "Supercalifragilisticexpialidocious"
4. Donna Karan
5. Better Business Bureau
6. Sand dollar

Red Light Challenge 1

Illinois
Indiana
Kentucky
North Carolina
Ohio
Virginia
West Virginia

7. Grace Kelly
8. Porsche

$100 questions

1. July 4th
2. Hemlock
3. Woolworth's
4. Windsor knot

Red Light Challenge 2

Louis Armstrong
Duke Ellington

AND THE ANSWERS ARE . . .

Ella Fitzgerald
Benny Goodman
Glenn Miller

5. Cousins
6. Toothpaste
7. Siam
8. Granny Smith

$200 questions

1. Falling Water
2. Mongolia
3. Freemasons
4. Seven
5. Falconry

Red Light Challenge 3

Cambodia
China
Laos
Myanmar (Burma)
Thailand
Vietnam

6. Tommy gun
7. Public places
8. Jason

Ben's Double or Nothing Bonus

Fiddler crab

AMSTERDAM AND 116TH
TO 81ST AND CENTRAL PARK WEST
(36 BLOCKS)

These questions are worth $50 each.

1. Let's start with a local New York institution. Once owned by Cornelius Vanderbilt, what

RED LIGHT CHALLENGE 1

Sometimes you hit a red light just as you pull away from the curb. As always, this Red Light Challenge is worth $250 and you have 30 seconds.

At Petfinder.com, the "small & furry" category includes eight different types of rodents. Name five of these eight species of pocket pets.

New York City boat service has been free of charge since 1997?

2. Caused by swollen salivary glands, "chipmunk cheeks" are a classic symptom of what common childhood illness?

3. In what temperature scale are the freezing and boiling points of water exactly 180 degrees apart?

4. What popular Chinese-American dish is named after a military leader from the Qing Dynasty?

5. In downhill skiing, what is the term for the hard mounds of snow designed to give racers a bumpy ride?

CENTRAL PARK SCULPTURE

There are twenty-nine statues in Central Park. They include composers (such as Duke Ellington, who stands beside a piano held up by naked ladies), liberators (including King Jagiello of Poland, who was actually Lithuanian), politicians (including John Purroy Mitchel—don't tell me you don't remember who he was!), innovators (including Dr. James Marion Sims, the founder of gynecology) and writers (including Hans Christian Andersen). And that's just the real people. There are also animals (including a dancing goat), angels, nymphs, fairies, characters from literature, iconic figures (such as a pilgrim and a falconer) and war memorials.

Which is Ben's favorite? Mother Goose at the entrance to the Rumsey Playfield. She's a nice old lady who knows how to tell a good story.

These questions are worth $100 each.

1. What Arabic network claims they're the only independent news outlet in the Middle East?
2. In 1994, Playtex unveiled what revolutionary push-up brassiere?
3. Often used for navigation, the celestial body Polaris is also known as what?
4. Of what famed FBI director was it said, "He always got his man, but he never found a woman"?
5. Colonists who sided with the British during the Revolutionary War were called what?

RED LIGHT CHALLENGE 2

This Red Light Challenge may prove to be a brain twister. Name four of the five states that average the highest number of tornados per year.
This is worth $250.

These questions are worth $200 each.

1. Swung like a sword, the Aztec *macana* was a club studded with sharp blades of what shiny volcanic rock?

2. Often stolen for its platinum, what smog-reducing car component can be ruined by leaded gasoline?

3. Glorified by the Beastie Boys, what primate-inspired cocktail mixes malt liquor with Sunny Delight?

4. What breed of hunting dog favored by photographer William Wegman is known for targeting its prey's privates?

5. Bajan, a mixture of Creole and English, is the language spoken by residents of what Caribbean nation?

WHERE DO CABBIES COME FROM?

Almost 90 percent of the cabdrivers in the New York metro area are foreign born. That's why you'll never go wrong asking a cabbie to recommend a good, cheap place to eat. This is especially true if you like Indian food or kebabs, because 23 percent of New York City's taxi and limo drivers are from Pakistan, India, and Bangladesh. But you'll get good recommendations for Caribbean food, too—20 percent are from the West Indies (primarily the Dominican Republic and Haiti).

If you're a fan of African food, though, you'll still get good recommendations. The number of cabdrivers from Egypt, Morocco, Ghana, and Nigeria is steadily increasing.

Ben's Double or Nothing Bonus

Familiar to fans of Jaws, the ominous fin on the back of a shark is called the dorsal fin. Meaning "tail" in Latin, what is the term for the speed-enhancing fin that brings up the rear?

AND THE ANSWERS ARE . . .

$50 questions

1. Staten Island Ferry

Red Light Challenge 1

Hamster
Rat
Mouse
Guinea pig
Gerbil
Chinchilla
Degu
Prairie dog

2. Mumps
3. Fahrenheit
4. General Tso's chicken
5. Moguls

$100 questions

1. Al Jazeera
2. Wonderbra
3. North Star
4. J. Edgar Hoover
5. Loyalists

Red Light Challenge 2

Texas
Oklahoma
Kansas

Florida
Nebraska

$200 questions

1. Obsidian
2. Catalytic converter
3. Brass monkey
4. Weimaraner
5. Barbados

Ben's Double or Nothing Bonus

Caudal (fin)

E 33rd St
E 32nd St
E 31st St
E 30th St
W 29th St
W 28th St
E 29th St
E 28th St
W 27th St
5th Ave
Avenue Of The Americas
W 25th St
Madison Square Park
Park Ave S
Lexington Ave
E 26th St
E 25th St
E 24th St
W 24th St
W 23rd St
W 22nd St
W 21st St
W 20th St
E 23rd St
E 22nd St
E 21st St
Gramercy Park
E 20th St
10th Ave
9th Ave
8th Ave
W 19th St
W 18th St
W 17th St
W 16th St
W 15th St
Broadway
Union Square
E 19th St
E 18th St
E 17th St
Stuyvesant Square
E 15th St
E 14th St
W 14th St
7th Ave
Irving Pl
Avenue C
1st Ave
Hudson St
W 12th St
W 13th St
E 13th St
University Pl
4th Ave
3rd Ave
E 11th St
E 12th St
Avenue B
Avenue A
W 11th St
7th Ave S
6th Ave
E 10th St
E 9th St
E 8th St
Tompkins Square Park
Bank St
Perry St
W 10th St
Christopher St
St Marks Pl
E 7th St
E 6th St
MacDougal St
Mercer St
W 3rd St
E 5th St
Lafayette St
Bowery
2nd Ave
E 4th St
E 3rd St
E 2nd St
Loisaida Ave
Morton St
Bleecker St
E 1st St
E Houston St
Clarkson St
Varick St
Stanton St
Prince St
Elizabeth St
Chrystie St
Rivington St
Pitt St
Greene St
Spring St
W Broadway
Allen St
Avenue Of The Immigrants
Ludlow St
Essex St
Broome St
Grand St
Mott St
Mulberry St
Canal St
E Broadway
Henry St
Laight St
Walker St
Hester St
Baxter St
Eldridge St
Seward Park
Beach St
White St
Centre St
Madison St
West St
Greenwich St
Leonard St
Worth St
Thomas Paine Park
Cherry St
E River Piers
Duane St
Chambers St
Park Row
Catherine St
Market St
Warren St
N End Ave
Governor Nelson A Rockefeller Park
City Hall Park
Franklin D Roosevelt Dr
Manhattan Brg
Murray St
Frankfort St
Church St
Vesey St
Ann St
Pearl St
Brooklyn Brg
North Cove
Liberty St
Nassau St
William St
Front St
South St
Albany St
278
E River Dr
Marginal St

WALL AND BROAD STREETS
TO WEST 4TH AND SIXTH AVENUE
(37 BLOCKS)

These questions are worth $50 each.

1. The home of Apple and Amazon, what high-tech stock market was shut down in 1994 due to outages caused by pesky squirrels?
2. Featuring dancing dolls in native costumes and a repeating theme song, what Disneyland ride has been compared to Dante's Sixth Circle of Hell?
3. What children's story features a lupine villain whose downfall is the structural superiority of bricks?
4. Although they're associated with the Wild West, what pesky windblown shrubs actually came to the United States via Ukraine?
5. According to her official bio, which game show sidekick claps her hands about 720 times per episode?

6. International Star Wars Day is held on May 4th, a date that alludes to what iconic Jedi greeting?

RED LIGHT CHALLENGE 1

According to USDA guidelines, what five fruits should be found in a can of fruit cocktail? You have 30 seconds to win $250.

These questions are worth $100 each.

1. The bass lover's best friend, what speaker component is used to reproduce the lowest audible frequencies?
2. Since the 1970s, what fast-food franchise has offered a sinus-clearing horseradish condiment called Horsey Sauce?
3. Popular with blues musicians, what style of guitar is played by pressing a small tube along the neck of the instrument?
4. The ball cock, invented by Thomas Crapper (you can't make this stuff up!), is a floating mechanism commonly found in what household fixture?
5. Not to be confused with Y2K, YKK is a Japanese company best known for manufacturing what type of fasteners?

6. Based on the work of Pythagoras, what occult offshoot of mathematics calculates the mystical meaning of digits?

TRINITY CHURCH

Trinity Church sits like a bishop at the head of Wall Street. It's the oldest Episcopal parish in New York—and the richest. In 1705, Queen Anne back in Britain granted the parish 215 acres of what was then farmland north of the city. Big land grants like that weren't uncommon in those days, but over the centuries churches mostly gave away or sold their land at whatever the price was at the time. Who knew real estate in Manhattan would one day be more precious than platinum?

Apparently, the church fathers at Trinity knew. The parish did lease some lots and give some away to other churches. But it held on to fifteen acres of the original 215. Most of it is now premium office space in SoHo. That pays for a lot of hymnals.

These questions are worth $200 each.

1. An omelet made with ham, onions, and green peppers is named for what Western city?
2. Giving birth to Exxon, Mobil, Chevron, and Conoco, what sprawling company was broken up in 1911 under the Sherman Antitrust Act?
3. At his request, what Hungarian-born horror film actor was buried in the black cape he wore as Dracula?

4. The Krugerrand gold coin was banned in many Western countries until the early 1990s. It is minted by what country?

RED LIGHT CHALLENGE 2

In Europe, six nations measure less than 200 square miles in area. For $250, name five of these teeny tiny countries.

5. What restaurant survey was created in 1979 by husband and wife team Tim and Nina?
6. If you paid rent to live in Ghent, you'd have neighbors in Flanders, a region of what country?

Ben's Double or Nothing Bonus

Always eager for a food fight, these lizards—the largest in the world—weaken their prey with a dose of deadly bacteria. Named for their island homeland, what is the name of these larger-than-life reptiles?

$50 questions

1. NASDAQ
2. "It's a Small World"
3. "Three Little Pigs"
4. Tumbleweeds
5. Vanna White
6. May the force be with you.

Red Light Challenge 1

Cherries
Grapes
Peaches
Pears
Pineapples

$100 questions

1. Woofer
2. Arby's
3. Slide (guitar)
4. Toilet
5. Zippers
6. Numerology

$200 questions

1. Denver
2. Standard Oil
3. Bela Lugosi
4. South Africa

AND THE ANSWERS ARE . . .

Red Light Challenge 2

Andorra
Liechtenstein
Malta
Monaco
San Marino
Vatican City

5. Zagat's
6. Belgium

Ben's Double or Nothing Bonus

Komodo dragon

GRAND CENTRAL STATION
TO 106TH AND THIRD AVENUE
(65 BLOCKS)

These questions are worth $50 each.

1. Due to their agile thumbs, what pesky, ringtailed scavengers can open garbage cans and turn doorknobs?
2. By what name was cigar-chomping comic Julius Henry Marx better known?
3. What U.S. government agency monitors insider trading violations and other investment fraud?
4. Made with mint, bourbon, sugar, and water, what is the traditional drink of the Kentucky Derby?
5. What famous stretch of ocean connecting Britain and France did Gertrude Ederle swim in 1926?
6. What TV chef popularized the exclamation "Bam!"?

RED LIGHT CHALLENGE 1

Our neighbor to the north consists of New Brunswick, Prince Edward Island, and eight other provinces, plus three territories. We're not getting territorial, but name five of the eight Canadian provinces. As always, this Red Light Challenge is worth $250 and you have 30 seconds.

7. Name the famed lingerie company that lifted its sales in 1993 by introducing the Miracle Bra.

8. What philosophical feline appears and disappears throughout *Alice in Wonderland*?

These questions are worth $100 each.

1. Meaning "extinction" in Sanskrit, what is the highest level of liberation and enlightenment a person can achieve in Buddhism?

2. What media mogul, born Down Under, runs News Corporation and its phalanx of Fox affiliates?

3. In the 1970s, the U.S. table tennis team made a historic "Ping Pong diplomacy" trip to what nation?

4. Based in Chicago, what comedy troupe's alumni include Bill Murray and Tina Fey?
5. The New York stadium that hosts the annual U.S. Open is named after what tennis legend?

RED LIGHT CHALLENGE 2

Here's a challenge to chew on. Since 1902, only four animals have remained constant staples of Barnum's Animal Crackers. Name all four of these bite-sized beasts.

6. Member countries of what policy-making organization control about two-thirds of the world's oil reserves?
7. What newspaper heiress and member of the Symbionese Liberation Army did President Bill Clinton pardon in 2001?
8. What New York landmark is over 1,400 feet tall and averages more than one hundred lightning strikes a year?

These questions are worth $200 each.

1. If you star in a horror movie and are afflicted with lycanthropy, what will you turn into?

TAXI OF TOMORROW

The largest number of taxis in New York are Ford Crown Victorias, but Ford announced a few years ago that they're phasing out that model. So for three years New York City was on the hunt for a new über cab that the Taxi and Limousine Commission gave the catchy name the Taxi of Tomorrow.

The idea was to award a single manufacturer an exclusive ten-year contract to provide all of the city's yellow cabs, starting in 2014. As older models wear out, eventually all of the city's 13,000 cabs will be replaced by the Taxi of Tomorrow.

The many entrants were narrowed down to three finalists, all small vans rather than cool Crown Victoria–like sedans: the Nissan NV200, currently made in Zhengzhou, China; the Ford Transit Connect, now made in Gölcük, Turkey; and the Karsan V-1, currently made in Bursa, Turkey.

The Taxi and Limousine Commission set up an elaborate Web site featuring the three cabs and invited New Yorkers to vote on their favorite. The Karsan won the popular vote. But in the end, the Nissan was crowned Taxi of Tomorrow and Karsan had to settle for the People's Choice Award. City officials decided they did not want to risk awarding the contract to a company with little experience in the American market—even though Karsan promised to build their assembly plant in Brooklyn.

The Nissan has a glass roof so everyone can enjoy New York's skyscrapers from the comfort of their cab, plus interior floor lighting, charging stations and USB ports for mobile devices, and independent, passenger-operated climate controls. It's not a hybrid engine, but the car can be converted to all-electric, and Nissan is working on a pilot project to test electric cabs in New York. The Taxi of Tomorrow will be assembled at Nissan's plant of today in Cuernavaca, Mexico—a long way from Brooklyn.

2. New York has some of the best pubs in the world. What is the term "pub" short for?

3. What 3,000-year-old dialect was supposedly spoken by Jesus and is the main language of the Talmud?

4. What did legendary lumberjack Paul Bunyan name his giant pet blue ox?

5. If you've just won a Clio Award, you've achieved excellence in what?

6. What common construction material is made from squares of gypsum sandwiched between two sheets of heavy paper?

7. If you're acrophobic, what exactly are you afraid of?

8. What is the official language of Liberia, Belize, and Zimbabwe?

GRAND CENTRAL TERMINAL

All around Grand Central Terminal are little decorative bits featuring acorns and oak leaves. Look around and you'll see them in the stonework of the water fountains, in the design of the chandeliers, above the entrance to the railroad tracks, and in the green metal window frames. It's a city squirrel's dream. What's the deal?

The acorn and oak tree were the symbols of choice—a kind of family crest—of railroad magnate Cornelius Vanderbilt. Vanderbilt built Grand Central Depot, the train station that came before Grand Central Terminal. The one that ran along Vanderbilt Avenue.

The richer Vanderbilt got, the more he felt like a European prince. So eventually he decided he needed a coat of arms. He chose the acorn and oak leaf, because "from an acorn a mighty oak shall grow."

Ben's Double or Nothing Bonus

Although farmers call it a dung beetle, this insect enjoyed sacred status among ancient Egyptians. From a Greek word meaning "crab," what is the common name for this symbolic six-legged creature?

AND THE ANSWERS ARE . . .

$50 questions

1. Raccoons
2. Groucho (Marx)
3. SEC (Securities and Exchange Commission)
4. Mint julep
5. English Channel
6. Emeril Lagasse

Red Light Challenge 1

Alberta
British Columbia
Manitoba
Newfoundland (and Labrador)
Nova Scotia
Ontario
Quebec
Saskatchewan

7. Victoria's Secret
8. Cheshire Cat

$100 questions

1. Nirvana
2. Rupert Murdoch
3. China
4. Second City
5. Arthur Ashe

Red Light Challenge 2

Bear
Elephant
Lion
Tiger

6. OPEC
7. Patty Hearst
8. Empire State Building

$200 questions

1. Werewolf
2. Public house
3. Aramaic
4. Babe
5. Advertising
6. Drywall
7. Heights
8. English

Ben's Double or Nothing Bonus

Scarab

PRINCE AND ELIZABETH STREETS
TO JANE AND GREENWICH
(29 BLOCKS)

These questions are worth $50 each.

1. Enjoyed hot or cold, what Japanese liquor was downed by kamikazes before they undertook their missions?
2. Often heard on *CSI*, the Latin phrase "post-mortem" means what in English?
3. What risqué style of bikini waxing did seven South American sisters first perform in the United States in 1987?
4. Founder Leon Leonwood put his initials in the name of what Maine-based clothing retailer?

These questions are worth $100 each.

1. What former Soviet Republic has the same name as a U.S. state?

POSH CAB

Taxi owners in New York are not allowed to just go out and buy whatever car they want, paint it yellow, install a meter, and hit the streets. The city's Taxi and Limousine Commission has a couple of approved models, and those are the only choices.

Currently, the approved models are the Ford Stretch Crown Victoria, Toyota Sienna, Ford Escape Hybrid, and, if you want a classier ride, Mercedes-Benz E350 Blutech. The Mercedes is a very recent addition to the list, and most cabdrivers have said there's no way they will fork over $51,000 to drive you around in a car that's nicer than the car they drive at home.

2. Which invertebrate uses a winning combination of mucous, suction, and anesthetic to feed off of its host?

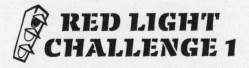

RED LIGHT CHALLENGE 1

We're stopped at a red light, and you know what that means.

In the Winnie-the-Pooh books, Christopher Robin and Pooh have seven animal friends. In 30 seconds, name five of their beastie pals.

3. Just across the river from New York City, what New Jersey town is thought to be the source of the word "hobo"?
4. What famous baseball bat brand has its own museum in Kentucky?

These questions are worth $200 each.

1. Developed by the founder of Bayer, what class of addictive sedatives was the downfall of both Marilyn Monroe and Jimi Hendrix?
2. Used to describe the tailbone and the appendix, what is the term for body parts that have become useless over the course of evolution?
3. Signed by more than five hundred assemblymen, the famed Tennis Court Oath sparked the beginning of what historic eighteenth-century event?
4. In Greek mythology, whose wings of wax melt off when he flies too close to the sun?

RED LIGHT CHALLENGE 2

Sitcom finales always draw big audiences—sometimes even audiences as big as Cash Cab's. Name four of the five sitcoms with the highest-rated series finales in TV history.
   This is worth $250.

Ben's Double or Nothing Bonus

Moose look pretty tough, but the word itself is from an Eastern Algonquian language and actually means "twig eater." This two-ton animal is all vegetarian. What country is home to the largest number of moose in the world?

$50 questions

1. Sake
2. After death
3. Brazilian wax
4. LLBean

$100 questions

1. Georgia
2. Leech

Red Light Challenge 1

Eeyore
Kanga
Owl
Piglet
Rabbit
Roo
Tigger

3. Hoboken
4. Louisville Slugger

$200 questions

1. Barbiturates
2. Vestigial
3. French Revolution
4. Icarus

AND THE ANSWERS ARE . . .

Red Light Challenge 2

*M*A*S*H

Cheers

Seinfeld

Friends

The Cosby Show

Ben's Double or Nothing Bonus

Canada

FIFTH AVENUE AND 59TH STREET
TO PARK AVENUE AND 23RD STREET
(39 BLOCKS)

These questions are worth $50 each.

1. What offshoot of the Gap, originally named for a bar in Paris, is known for its kitschy commercials and high-performance fleece?
2. Also an NFL team, what dark-feathered cousin of the crow did Native Americans revere as a god of creation and trickery?
3. In the 1980s, Bud Light fans were shocked to learn that what "sly ladies-dog" was actually female?
4. In the Revolutionary War, what sharp rifle attachments did American soldiers often use as makeshift cooking skewers?
5. Famously favored by James Bond, what method of martini preparation is said to result in a watered-down, cloudy cocktail?

NEED A JOB?

If you're looking for a new occupation where you can set your own hours and be your own boss, consider becoming a cabbie. The Bureau of Labor Statistics says the number of cabdriver jobs is projected to increase 13 percent through 2016. Las Vegas has the fastest-growing population of drivers, but Boston and New York are not far behind.

These questions are worth $100 each.

1. In the world of radio broadcasting (and even on the radio in the Cash Cab), "AM" is an abbreviation for amplitude modulation. What does "FM" stand for?
2. Traditionally, a diamond commemorates a seventy-fifth wedding anniversary. What material commemorates a one-year anniversary?

RED LIGHT CHALLENGE 1

This Red Light Challenge rewards thinking big. According to the U.S. Census Bureau, what are five of the eight countries with the largest populations as of 2010?

3. Providing oxygen to the body's tissues, what blood vessels are so tiny that red blood cells travel through them single file?

4. Used to paralyze prey, the metasoma is the venomous, stinging tail of what desert-dwelling arachnid?

5. Neither Dionne Warwick nor her pals predicted the 1998 bankruptcy of what famous fortune-telling phone service?

THE PLAZA HOTEL

The Plaza Hotel, where this trip starts, is one of those places where everyone famous has stayed: F. Scott and Zelda Fitzgerald, Ernest Hemingway, Frank Lloyd Wright, Eleanor Roosevelt, Groucho Marx, Truman Capote, The Beatles, and Crocodile Dundee. Eartha Kitt and Peggy Lee, two very smooth women, both played the Persian Room at the Plaza.

The Plaza represents one of those weird, "only in New York" real estate deals: It's jointly owned by Elad Properties, an Israeli company, and Kingdom Holdings, a Saudi Arabian firm. Money, it seems, is the great unifier.

These questions are worth $200 each.

1. A relative of the harp, what ancient Greek instrument traditionally consisted of strings attached to a tortoise shell?

2. The only Confederate soldier convicted of war crimes, Henry Wirz was commandant of what infamous Civil War prison?

3. Associated with the Wild West, what slang term for "scram" is derived from a Spanish word meaning "let's go"?
4. Sharing their name with a fabled Brooklyn pizzeria, the Grimaldis are the ruling family of what European principality?
5. The Shaolin monastery, located in Henan Province in China, is the birthplace of what ancient martial art?

RED LIGHT CHALLENGE 2

The first Winter Olympics, held in 1924, featured just seven events. Name five of these seven original cold-weather sports. Remember, this is worth $250 and you have 30 seconds.

Ben's Double or Nothing Bonus

Orchids aren't just for Mother's Day. In Madagascar, vast orchid plantations produce over half of the world's supply of what flavorful bean?

$50 questions

1. Old Navy
2. Raven
3. Spuds Mackenzie
4. Bayonets
5. Shaken, not stirred (the right answer includes both)

$100 questions

1. Frequency modulation
2. Paper

Red Light Challenge 1

China
India
United States
Indonesia
Brazil
Pakistan
Bangladesh
Nigeria

3. Capillaries
4. Scorpion
5. Psychic Friends Network

$200 questions

1. Lyre
2. Andersonville

AND THE ANSWERS ARE . . .

3. Vamoose
4. Monaco
5. Kung fu

Red Light Challenge 2

Biathlon
Bobsled
Curling
Figure skating
Ice hockey
Skiing
Speed skating

Ben's Double or Nothing Bonus

Vanilla

COLUMBUS CIRCLE
TO 23RD AND MADISON
(39 BLOCKS)

These questions are worth $50 each.

1. According to a famous couplet by Dorothy
   Parker, "Men seldom make passes at girls
   who" do what?
2. Taken every ten years, the U.S. Census is
   used to reallocate seats for what specific
   legislative body?

RED LIGHT CHALLENGE 1

*Time to show off your higher learning in this Red
Light Challenge. Name six of the eight venerable
institutions that make up the Ivy League.*

3. Abbreviated "NVG," what optical instruments use infrared light to help soldiers see in the dark?

4. What depressing national park spanning California and Nevada is home to such grim rock formations as Dante's View and the Devil's Golf Course?

5. Involving the placement of foreign objects in the skin, a scratch test is used to diagnose what physical condition?

6. Gotham City has Batman and New York has the Cash Cab. What fictional city does Superman call home?

These questions are worth $100 each.

1. The Bible has been translated into more than 1,100 languages, including what fictional *Star Trek* language?

2. Welcome to *Law & Order: Cash Cab.* In a trial, what is the term for a conference between the judge and the lawyers that is not heard by the jury?

3. What African-American track star made history at the 1936 Berlin Olympics by winning four gold medals?

4. Lending the word "sauna" to the English language, Suomi is the official tongue of what Scandinavian country?

5. Played by more than 6 million people, "World of Warcraft" is a massive, multiplayer online RPG. What is "RPG" an abbreviation for?

6. In 2007, who became the first person to be nominated for both an Academy Award and a Nobel Prize in the same year?

MADISON SQUARE PARK

At the southeast corner of Madison Square Park, where this ride ends, is a statue of Senator Roscoe Conkling, the leader of the New York State Republican Party in the 1870s. He froze to death at that very spot during the great 1888 blizzard, after refusing to pay $50 for a cab ride home. There's a lesson here for stubborn senators everywhere, but blame the cabbie, too. In 1888 you could buy six really good cows for $500 and a worker in the garment industry earned between $250 and $350 in a year, so $50 for a cab ride was pretty outrageous, even in a blizzard.

These questions are worth $200 each.

1. In the U.S. Marine Corps, what is the lowest rank a soldier can have?

RED LIGHT CHALLENGE 2

Cape Fear *and* Casino *are two movies directed by Martin Scorsese that star Robert DeNiro. Name four others.*

This is worth $250 and you've got 30 seconds.

2. In music, what term describes a male voice singing in an upper register beyond his normal range?
3. Name the cold and calculating Renaissance philosopher who wrote *The Prince*.
4. Including the cue ball, how many billiard balls are used in a traditional game of eight ball?
5. What ballet move is defined as a dancer doing a complete body turn on the toes?
6. With values from 1 to 5, the Saffir-Simpson scale measures the strength of what?

Ben's Double or Nothing Bonus

Immortalized by painter Paul Gauguin, this surfer's paradise is a hot spot for well-heeled honeymooners. A stone's throw from Bora Bora, what is the name of this idyllic Polynesian island?

AND THE ANSWERS ARE . . .

$50 questions

1. Wear glasses
2. House of Representatives

Red Light Challenge 1

Brown (University)
Columbia (University)
Cornell (University)
Dartmouth (College)
Harvard (University)
University of Pennsylvania
Princeton (University)
Yale (University)

3. Night-vision goggles
4. Death Valley
5. Allergies
6. Metropolis

$100 questions

1. Klingon
2. Sidebar
3. Jesse Owens
4. Finland
5. Role-playing game
6. Al Gore

$200 questions

1. Private

Red Light Challenge 2

Goodfellas
Mean Streets
New York, New York
Raging Bull
Taxi Driver
The King of Comedy

2. Countertenor
3. (Niccolò) Machiavelli
4. Sixteen
5. Pirouette
6. Hurricanes

Ben's Double or Nothing Bonus

Tahiti

SIXTH AVENUE AND CARMINE STREET
TO 84TH AND FIFTH AVENUE
(80 BLOCKS)

These questions are worth $50 each.

1. Let's start with a drink. What liquor is added to coffee to make it an Irish coffee?
2. What popular brand of plastic kitchenware features the Wonder Bowl with its "burping seal"?
3. In what U.S. state could the Cash Cab drive you all the way from the Panhandle to the Keys?
4. What type of orphaned animal would a ranch hand corral by saying, "Get along, little doggie"?
5. Known simply as "The Great One," what hockey legend retired from the NHL in 1999?
6. In 1945, what toy did a naval engineer accidentally create when his tension spring fell down the stairs?

7. In Indian cuisine, naan and chapati are two types of what basic food?
8. The Cold War boundary between communist and noncommunist Europe was called "The Iron" what?

RED LIGHT CHALLENGE 1

Our first Red Light Challenge.
In 30 seconds, name four of the six actors who have been on Her Majesty's Secret Service, playing 007 in the official James Bond feature films.

9. Believing the bald eagle to be of "bad moral character," Benjamin Franklin lobbied for what feathered fowl to be our national bird?
10. Mariana is not a type of sauce, but the deepest trench on Earth, found in what ocean?

These questions are worth $100 each.

1. What figure of speech combines two contradictory terms, such as "deafening silence?"
2. Latin for "seeded apple," what trendy fruit is thought to have more antioxidant properties than green tea?
3. Name the lucky Pulitzer Prize–winning playwright who married Marilyn Monroe in 1956.

4. The hook-and-ladder, Statue of Liberty, and fumblerooski are trick plays used in what sport?

5. Once home to Three Rivers Stadium, in what city do the Allegheny, Monongahela, and Ohio Rivers meet?

RED LIGHT CHALLENGE 2

Time to become the next Mr. Moneybags. Name the four railroads for sale in the original version of the Parker Brothers game Monopoly.

6. Meaning "thigh" in Latin, what is the largest and strongest bone in the human body?

7. Now six bucks a trip, twenty-five cents used to get you one ride on what eighty-year-old Coney Island roller coaster?

8. What notorious serial killer murdered his victims in the Whitechapel region of London in 1888?

9. Typified by a large cranium, what species of early man roamed Europe and western Asia more than thirty thousand years ago?

10. Sojourner, Spirit, and Opportunity are unmanned vehicles famous for their missions where?

BEN'S FAVORITE NEW YORK TRIANGLES

Father Demo Square

Despite the name, this is really a triangle in Greenwich Village, where Bleecker Street crosses Sixth Avenue (Avenue of the Americas, for those of you who are from out of town). I love this quiet sliver of a park. It's a great place for people watching, or just sitting and looking up at the trees.

The Flatiron Building

This iconic building wedged in where Broadway, Fifth Avenue, and 23rd Street meet is just six feet wide at the apex. When it was completed in 1902, it was the world's tallest skyscraper at a whopping twenty-one stories or 305 feet.

TriBeCa

The Triangle Below Canal Street has great art galleries, interesting restaurants, and some of New York's best industrial-historical architecture. Plus, Robert DeNiro lives down here, and he starred in my favorite movie, *Taxi Driver*.

Automotive Bermuda Triangle Around the Empire State Building

There's a five-block radius around the Empire State Building where cars mysteriously won't start. Nobody is exactly sure why, but the 203-foot-long antenna at the top of the iconic building is the prime suspect. Automotive experts and engineers think it's jamming the remote keyless entry systems of some cars. This is yet another reason to leave your car at home and take a cab around Manhattan.

Worth Square

Another square that's a triangle, this one is at 25th Street right where Broadway and Fifth Avenue cross, next to Madison Square

Park. There's an obelisk here honoring General William Jenkins Worth, for whom Fort Worth, Texas, was named, as well as Worth Street in lower Manhattan. What makes this an interesting spot? Worth is actually buried underneath the monument.

These questions are worth $200 each.

1. Named for its Italian inventor, what blood-colored brand of aperitif has made cocktails bitter since 1860?
2. The chief component of cell walls in plants, what substance can be digested by cows and termites, but not humans?
3. Also an apt motto for *Cash Cab*, what one-word slogan did IBM president Thomas Watson post throughout his company's offices?
4. Familiar to fans of *Star Trek*, what alliterative ability enables Mr. Spock to share his memories with a single touch?

RED LIGHT CHALLENGE 3

Think back to 1975 when Saturday Night Live *was always funny and name five members of that original cast.*
This is worth $250.

5. Used to bludgeon armor, what centuries-old weapon was basically a club topped with a spiked metal head?

6. With a population of under five hundred, what rare subspecies of tiger is named for the Indonesian island it calls home?

7. Often associated with the Greek god Pan, what mythological creature is known for its irrepressible sex drive?

8. Jackie Joyner-Kersee is arguably the most famous athlete to earn a gold medal in what seven-event Olympic sport?

9. When not preoccupied with peanuts, George Washington Carver also found one hundred eighteen uses for what starchy tuber?

10. Nicknamed Muttnik, what famous canine cosmonaut did the Soviet Union send into space in 1957?

IT'S A GUY THING

While a cab is a great way to take a woman home from a date, it's not a great place to meet one. Only about 3 percent of all New York metro area cabdrivers are women.

Ben's Double or Nothing Bonus

It's obvious why they call New York the greatest city on earth. Before the British renamed this magnificent metropolis New York City, what did the Dutch call it?

AND THE ANSWERS ARE . . .

$50 questions

1. Whiskey
2. Tupperware
3. Florida
4. Calf
5. (Wayne) Gretzky
6. Slinky
7. Bread
8. Curtain

Red Light Challenge 1

Sean Connery
George Lazenby
Roger Moore
Timothy Dalton
Pierce Brosnan
Daniel Craig

9. Turkey
10. Pacific Ocean

$100 questions

1. Oxymoron
2. Pomegranate
3. Arthur Miller
4. Football
5. Pittsburgh

Red Light Challenge 2

Reading (Railroad)
Pennsylvania (Railroad)
B&O (Railroad)
Short Line (Railroad)

6. Femur
7. The Cyclone
8. Jack the Ripper
9. Neanderthal
10. Mars

$200 questions

1. Campari
2. Cellulose
3. "Think"
4. Mind meld

Red Light Challenge 3

Dan Aykroyd
John Belushi
Chevy Chase
Jane Curtin
Garret Morris
Laraine Newman
Gilda Radner

5. Mace
6. Sumatran
7. Satyr
8. Heptathlon

9. Sweet potato
10. Laika

Ben's Double or Nothing Bonus

New Amsterdam

W 31st St
E 33rd St
E 32nd St
E 31st St
E 30th St
W 29th St
W 28th St
E 29th St
E 28th St
W 27th St
5th Ave
Avenue Of The Americas
W 25th St
W 24th St
Madison Square Park
Park Ave S
Lexington Ave
E 26th St
E 25th St
E 24th St
W 23rd St
W 22nd St
W 21st St
W 20th St
E 23rd St
E 22nd St
E 21st St
E 23rd St
10th Ave
9th Ave
8th Ave
Broadway
Gramercy Park
E 20th St
W 19th St
W 18th St
W 17th St
W 16th St
W 15th St
E 19th St
E 18th St
E 17th St
7th Ave
Union Square
Irving Pl
Stuyvesant Square
E River Dr
Marginal St
E River Piers
Avenue C
W 14th St
E 15th St
E 14th St
E 14th St
E 15th St
Hudson St
Washington St
W 12th St
W 13th St
E 13th St
4th Ave
3rd Ave
1st Ave
E 11th St
E 12th St
W 11th St
7th Ave S
6th Ave
5th Ave
University Pl
E 10th St
E 9th St
E 8th St
Avenue A
Avenue B
Avenue C
Bank St
Perry St
W 10th St
Christopher
MacDougal St
St Marks Pl
E 7th St
Tompkins Square Park
E 8th St
E 6th St
E 5th St
E 4th St
E 3rd St
E 2nd St
W 3rd St
Mercer St
Lafayette St
Bowery
2nd Ave
Loisaida Ave
Morton St
Bleecker St
Bleecker St
Clarkson St
E 1st St
E Houston St
Hamilton Fish
Varick St
Hudson St
6th Ave
W Broadway
Greene St
Broadway
Prince St
Spring St
Elizabeth St
Chrystie St
Avenue Of The Immigrants
Stanton St
Rivington St
Ludlow St
Pitt St
Broome St
Broome St
Grand St
Grand St
Mott St
Mulberry St
Allen St
Essex St
Eldridge St
Canal St
Laight St
Beach St
Walker St
Hester St
Baxter St
Centre St
E Broadway
Henry St
Seward Park
White St
Leonard St
Worth St
Duane St
Thomas Paine Park
N River Piers
West St
Greenwich St
Madison St
Cherry St
Catherine St
Bayard St
Market St
E River Piers
FDR
Chambers St
Warren St
N End Ave
Park Row
City Hall Park
Governor Nelson A Rockefeller Park
Murray St
Church St
Frankfort St
Franklin D Roosevelt Dr
Manhattan Brg
Vesey St
Ann St
Pearl St
Brooklyn Brg
North Cove
Liberty St
Albany St
Trinity
Heroes
Nassau St
William St
Pearl St
Front St
South St
Pine St
Esplanade
278
9

FIRST AVENUE AND 9TH STREET
TO 29TH AND TENTH
(31 BLOCKS)

These questions are worth $50 each.

1. Not just for contact lenses, what alternative to silicone was adopted by breast implant manufacturers in 1962?
2. Despite his penchant for shooting communists, what Sylvester Stallone role is said to be a favorite of Kim Jong-Il?
3. For those who disdain dairy, what essential nutrient can also be found in molasses, sardines, and ground-up eggshells?
4. Later stripped of her medal, Rosie Ruiz used the subway to win what iconic New England event in 1980?
5. Also a type of Cuban drum, what kitschy line dance features the sequence: step, step, step, kick?

These questions are worth $100 each.

1. In 2006, the State Department began implanting radio frequency chips in what government-issued document?
2. A famously prolific father, what Mongol leader's Y-chromosome is thought to be carried by more than sixteen million men?
3. In 1712, Czar Peter the Great moved the capital of Russia from Moscow to what northern city?
4. In 2004, what British company announced plans to take tourists on suborbital space flights for a proposed cost of $200,000 apiece?

RED LIGHT CHALLENGE 1

There's a lot of monkey business going on outside this cab, but only seven mammals are officially considered to be apes. Name four of them in 30 seconds.

5. What "royal" reptile can grow up to seventeen feet long, making it the largest venomous snake in the world?

These questions are worth $200 each.

1. What Nintendo video game features two siblings fighting evil in the Mushroom Kingdom?
2. What musical pioneer born in 1915 has a popular Gibson guitar named for him?
3. Mohair is a fabric made from the hair of what animal?
4. During halftime of what sport do spectators dash onto the field for a "divot stomp?"
5. What former president once said, "You can tell a lot about a fellow's character by his way of eating jelly beans"?

RED LIGHT CHALLENGE 2

In tennis, what four tournaments make up the Grand Slam? This is worth $250 (considerably less than you'd earn winning a Grand Slam tournament).

Ben's Double or Nothing Bonus

When bats hang around, they leave behind drop-pings used to make everything from fertilizer to gunpowder. Derived from a Quechua (the language of the Incas) word, what term is commonly used to refer to this bat waste?

$50 questions

1. Saline
2. Rambo
3. Calcium
4. Boston Marathon
5. Conga

$100 questions

1. Passport
2. Genghis Khan
3. St. Petersburg
4. Virgin

Red Light Challenge 1

Bonobo
Chimpanzee
Gibbon
Gorilla
Human
Orangutan
Siamang

5. King cobra

$200 questions

1. Super Mario Brothers
2. Les Paul
3. Goat

AND THE ANSWERS ARE . . .

4. Polo
5. Ronald Reagan

Red Light Challenge 2

Australian Open
French Open
U.S. Open
Wimbledon

Ben's Double or Nothing Bonus

Guano

AVENUE C AND 12TH STREET
TO BOWERY AND CANAL
(22 BLOCKS)

These questions are worth $50 each.

1. Also known as a three-leaf clover, what is the official symbol of Ireland's Aer Lingus?
2. In the music genre known as R&B, what does "R&B" stand for?

RED LIGHT CHALLENGE 1

Ten states line the banks of the Mississippi River, including Mississippi and Louisiana. Name six of the other eight states. You have 30 seconds to win $250 here.

3. Associated with granola eaters, what brand of sandals traces its roots back to an eighteenth-century German cobbler?
4. Named for their devout posture, what insects are known for their violent ritual of the female biting off the male's head after mating?

THE EAST RIVER BRIDGES

As any cabbie will tell you, coming or going from Manhattan, you always have to pay. Except on the East River bridge crossings—the Brooklyn, Manhattan, and Williamsburg Bridges, and the 59th Street Bridge. There are always plans on the table to put toll plazas on those bridges, and they somehow always get defeated.

If you have a hard time remembering the order of the bridges that connect lower Manhattan with Brooklyn, just imagine you're a German tourist; working your way uptown, it's BMW—Brooklyn, Manhattan, Williamsburg.

These questions are worth $100 each.

1. Businessman Henry Phillips invented and lent his name to an easy-to-use variety of what tool?
2. What famed circus impresario did fellow carney James Bailey team up with in 1881?
3. According to legend, the phrase "sent up the river" refers to doing time in what New York State prison?
4. If a Hawaiian says "mahalo," what is he saying in English?

These questions are worth $200 each.

1. Sported by Rambo and Chewbacca, what type of ammunition belt is strapped across the chest?
2. Practiced by Plato, what philosophical process is based on an exchange of arguments called the thesis and antithesis?

RED LIGHT CHALLENGE 2

Four U.S. presidents were assassinated while in office. Name these four unlucky commanders in chief.

3. Immortalized in a Christmas carol, what "Good King" is also the patron saint of the Czech Republic?
4. What synonym for "nerd" is a reference to the bespectacled scientist in the Felix the Cat cartoons?

ETYMOLOGY

Taxicab is a combination of two words. The taximeter was invented in 1891, and is an instrument used to measure both the distance and time a car has traveled. The cabriolet is a light, two-wheeled carriage drawn by one horse. Put them all together and they spell taxicab.

Ben's Double or Nothing Bonus

Despite the fact that it has the same name, this historic Spanish city is unlikely to be mistaken for an industrial town in Ohio. An early center of religious and cultural tolerance, what is the name of this former Spanish capital?

$50 questions

1. Shamrock
2. Rhythm & blues

Red Light Challenge 1

Arkansas
Illinois
Iowa
Kentucky
Minnesota
Missouri
Tennessee
Wisconsin

3. Birkenstocks
4. Praying mantis

$100 questions

1. Screwdriver
2. P. T. Barnum
3. Sing Sing
4. Thank you

$200 questions

1. Bandolier
2. Dialectics

AND THE ANSWERS ARE . . .

Red Light Challenge 2

Abraham Lincoln
James Garfield
William McKinley
John F. Kennedy

3. Wenceslas
4. Poindexter

Ben's Double or Nothing Bonus

Toledo